CHISNELL ON
INSTRUMENT TECHNIQUES

CHISNELL ON INSTRUMENT TECHNIQUES

Mark Chisnell

WATERLINE

Published by Waterline Books
an imprint of Airlife Publishing Ltd
101 Longden Rd, Shrewsbury, England

ISBN 1 85310 311 X

A Sheerstrake production.

A CIP catalogue record of this book
is available from the British Library

Contents

Introduction

At the beginning of the 1980's this book would have had no place in the racing navigator's library. But a rule change that allowed electronics onto boats, advances in modern technology and a different type of racing have all helped alter the navigator's job to the point where it is almost a misnomer. Not totally, because, if only for safeties sake, there will always be a need for the traditional skills of chart work and position fixing. But if we assume that the equipment remains working, then 'navigation', in a world where your position flashes up on a display to within 100 metres, is something anyone can do. This is particularly true of the racing that is currently most popular – inshore Olympic style courses where water depth is no more relevant than to a dinghy sailor, and your position is only important in the context of the tactical situation. In the 1990's the problem begins with the position: how can it be most effectively processed, so that it utilizes the myriad other data that comes bubbling out of the electronics, to its greatest effect?

This is the problem to which this book is devoted. There are many excellent works on the more traditional aspects of navigation, and more are published all the time. So we shall leave to these others the intricacies of charts, dividers and sextants and concentrate on what will most profit the modern race boat navigator – how to get the right information out of the electronic equipment to help the boat win races.

In a sense we will define a new role for the 'navigator' (or whatever it is we should now call him). A role which will enable him to contribute to success, or failure, on the race course in a lot more ways than was possible ten years ago. Jobs, like data collection and performance analysis, that were scarcely possible then, but which now, for the investment of some time and effort, can make the navigator's role both more interesting and valuable.

We will be concentrating on the equipment normally used in the mainstream of yacht racing; position fixing and instrument systems. Whilst radar, autopilots and weather satellite systems all have parts to play in specialised races, they are of little direct consequence to those of us who do not wish, or have no opportunity, to race round the world or across oceans. Of these two, the instrument system provides the greatest challenge. Everyone aboard a racing yacht will use the instrument system at some time or another. Tacticians for wind information, helmsmen and trimmers for boat speed, and mast-men to gauge the time to the next sail change. But someone must be responsible for this information, its accuracy, collection, assimilation, comparison to what has gone before and projection into what lies ahead. This is the job description of the navigator, and the contents of this book.

Position Fixing Systems

Some thoughts

Fixing your position accurately, in relation to both the nearest land and the race course, was for a long time the essence of being a good navigator. Knowing where you were as you hurtled towards a lee shore finish line in thirty five knots, with the 1.5 oz up and a night whose blackness is only relieved by the luminescence of the white horses, was no joke before the advent of electronic position fixing systems. In these days of the Global Positioning System (GPS) the problem is almost (but not quite) trivial. The skills of good position fixing now mainly consist of finding the power switch.

Of the four main navigation systems, for the type of racing we are concerned with here, Decca and Loran just about meet the specifications in terms of accuracy and update rate. Transit Satellite Navigation (Satnav) suffers badly from its update rate. Tracking lay lines up a three mile beat with fixes only every half an hour is not going to work, but if you are going offshore and out of range of Loran or Decca, then you may need to consider Satnav as well. Of course if you buy both, you might just as well go for a GPS set instead and be done with the whole problem. In every respect GPS is superior, but it is also more expensive, at least in the short term. However, as with all electronic equipment, the price is dropping. Its increasing price accessibility and superior performance should quickly make it the world's premier navigation system. But for a while the other three systems – Loran, Decca and Satnav – still have their place.

In the rest of this chapter we have outlined the workings of these four navigation systems. Loran, Decca and Satnav are dealt with rather more briefly, since they have been around long enough for there to be a great deal of published information already available. Also, as we have already mentioned, as GPS becomes more popular we can expect them to be of increasingly little importance. For the same reasons the section on GPS is more detailed.

With each of these systems you will need to know their limitations and also how to push them to their extremes. As a navigator you want latitude and longitude and some idea of its accuracy, combined with a relatively easy means of converting this into something more useful such as cross track error or speed over the ground. The advice that follows is, of necessity, general. The in-depth practical detail can only come from the manual and whatever is said about it being the last resort – you should read it. What we are really interested in here, is how to use this information to help you win races, and this is the topic of the final section of the chapter.

Decca and Loran

Decca and Loran are both hyperbolic navigation systems (hyperbolic refers to the shape of the lines of position) working from land-based radio signals. A network of transmitters provides timed radio signals from which the receivers can calculate lines of position and hence triangulate a position. Between them they provide a coastal navigation system for most of the western world. Decca covers the English Channel, the Atlantic coasts of France and Britain, the North Sea and Baltic coasts of Northern Europe and Scandinavia. There are further chains in South Africa, Japan, the Gulf and parts of India. Loran is more widespread, covering all the North American seaboards, Hawaii, Japan, the Philippines, North Atlantic, Mediterranean and the Middle East.

Decca works by the emission of radio signals in phase from each of the transmitters, by which we mean that the peaks of the radio wave are sent at exactly the same time. So the amount they are out of phase by the time they reach the receiver defines the relative distance to each transmitter. From two transmitters you can calculate a line of position;. A third transmitter then combines with one of the others to provide a second line of position (LOP). The principle transmitter involved in both LOP's is usually called the Master.

The modern Decca receiver works all this out for you, and from its received radio signals you will see a latitude and longitude which it presents with a disconcerting degree of certainty. This is part of the problem, since there is little indication of the accuracy of the information and much of the skill in using a Decca receiver lies in knowing when it can be trusted. Many of the various factors affecting the accuracy are dependent in some way on the workings of the system, so you should have some idea of what goes into producing those numbers.

The first factor you should consider is your distance from the transmitter. As we can see from Diagram 1.1, the further you are away, then the wider apart the LOPs become for the same gap in phase difference. So for the same accuracy of time measurement you get considerably less accuracy of position. The variation will be of the order of 50 metres at 500–1000 metres from a transmitter and 500 metres accuracy at 300 kilometres from a transmitter. This is about the limit of the effective range of a Decca transmitter. All these distances are dependent on the conditions and should not be taken as anything more than guides.

It is not only the distance from transmitters that is important , but also your position relative to them. Watch out for the crossing angle of the LOPs, the closer the angle is to 90 degrees — the greater the accuracy will be. What you need here are charts where the transmitters and the LOPs derived from them are shown. You can see both the spacing and the angle of contact — information you need to make a judgement on the accuracy of your position.

Equally critical are the areas near a baseline extension. The baseline is the line running directly between two transmitters, the baseline extension being the extension of that line past the transmitter. Any fixes you get in this area are unreliable in the direction of the baseline — but accurate at right angles to it.

13

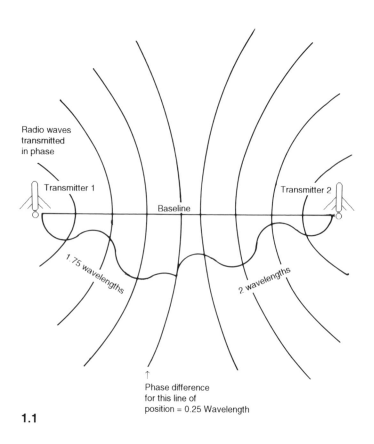

1.1

Another factor is distortion of the signal, since it is refracted when it passes over land. This is particularly tricky since the error will vary seasonally, as trees lose and gain leaves for instance. Again, you will need an appreciation of where the transmitters are, and the amount and terrain of the land between you and them, to have any idea of the type of errors that may be induced. There is also a variation due to the time of day because the propagation of the signal changes; once the sun goes down.

Combine all this with such random effects as noise, weak signals, atmospheric interference etc. and it is a wonder that the system works at all. Of course it does, and it works remarkably well. The number of times I have sailed out to the middle of the English Channel in search of the remote buoy EC1 and found it exactly where the Decca said it would be, is 100%. Perhaps I am just lucky, but at a practical level it is hard not to give the impression that the Decca is really pretty reliable. After all, when you get close to a shoreline, where there are most likely to be errors, you tend to revert to other techniques anyway — visuals, depth and so on. Nevertheless, it pays to be aware of why Decca might be in error and when you should be cautious.

The capabilities of the particular model you have are important too. Does your Decca take into account the possible errors introduced by your position relative to the transmitters when it selects such transmitters? Does it have the facility to be forced onto another transmitter if it does not? If it tells you when the signal is unreliable, what effects does this take into account? You should understand the various options your Decca provides, chain overrides and signal strength; tweaks, all of which can be found in the manual.

The workings of Loran are much the same as for Decca. The main difference is that Loran works from the Time Difference (TD) of the pulsed signals it receives from the master and secondary transmitters, rather than the phase difference. The result is the same; two lines of position which can be converted into a latitude and longitude either by a chart marked up with both TD co-ordinates and latitude and longitude, or calculated by the receiver itself — which is the case in almost all modern units.

The errors that Loran is susceptible to are similar to Decca; crossing angles of the LOPs, baseline extension problems and so on. Loran does use a lower frequency than Decca and so the longer wavelength propagates further and is more stable. The consequence is greater range, perhaps up to 800 miles from the Loran chain and greater repeatability of position fix — maybe as good as 30 metres. It also means that the beacons can be further apart in each chain. The advantage of this is that errors or jumps in position which you see with Decca as you move from one chain to the other are much rarer with Loran. The disadvantage is that the grid of time differences is more spread out, which reduces the overall theoretical accuracy of Loran to less than that of Decca — given the same distance from the transmitters. A factor which is probably more than compensated for by the more stable propagation of the waves.

The refractive distortion of the signal by the land is also the same as for Decca. Some Loran units come with corrections programmed in, where they have been charted, others allow you to program them in yourself. By comparing chart positions with the Loran position, in fair weather, you can work out the error and then enter it as a permanent correction. It is a particularly useful function and as with Decca you will need to have a good grasp of the in's and out's of your unit to be able to use these facilities effectively on the race course. Everything mentioned about Decca usage applies here.

Transit Satellite Navigation

The principal limitation of both Loran and Decca, apart from accuracy, is their localised coverage — they only work where there are land based chains of beacons to provide the signal. This limits their use to the coastal zones and therefore neither Decca nor Loran are of much use for blue water sailing. A system that overcomes this problem, but which has a low position update rate that severely limits its use inshore, is Transit Satellite Navigation or Satnav. In some ways it is peripheral to the type of racing we are considering here, which almost by definition takes place within range of Loran or Decca. If your racing is remote and you need this system, you would be better off with GPS. But, for completeness and for those who already have the equipment, we will cover it.

Transit Satnav works on a different principle altogether — the Doppler shift. As one object moves past another, the frequency of any transmission from it, as measured by the stationary object, changes. This is because of the velocity added to and then removed from the transmission by the objects approach and departure (see Diagram 1.2). It can be observed when a motorbike approaches and passes you; the pitch of the engine noise will change as it does so. Satnav uses the Doppler shift to fix the position of an object on the ground from the transmission of a passing satellite. The Transit Satnav system is a set of seven polar orbiting satellites circling the earth every 107 minutes at an altitude of less than 700 miles. The orbits are fixed so that the earth rotates in a sort of cage beneath them. Every time a satellite appears over the horizon to your Satnav antenna, the microprocessor inside the connected box receives information from it, measures the Doppler shift and calculates your position. This has the major advantage over Loran and Decca of working anywhere in the world. The problem is that the satellites can take between 35 minutes and six hours to appear, depending on your latitude — the cage widens its bars the nearer you are to the equator.

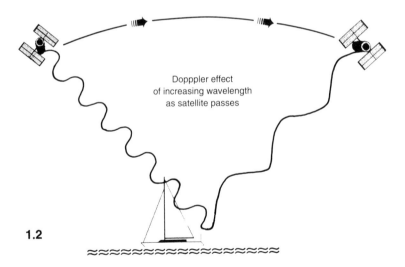

Dopppler effect
of increasing wavelength
as satellite passes

1.2

To a certain extent this can be overcome by the use of a dead reckoning system to keep the boats position updated between satellite fixes. The boat's speed and heading can be either manually input or fed in from the instrument system. Apart from providing a continuous record of position, this has the more important task of allowing the Satnav to account for the yacht's motion in its calculation of the Doppler shift. Small errors in the yacht's velocity can lead to quite large errors in the position. If the yacht's speed is input to the calculation accurately, then Satnav can provide a good fix. Its limitation to the racing sailor, is that you do not get this fix very often. On the up side, the satellite sends out its signals in the VHF and UHF region and these are unaffected by weather, time of day, season, ionospheric variations, or just about anything — so long as the satellite is in line of sight of the aerial, as required by these short wavelength radio signals.

Global Positioning System

The Global Positioning System, or GPS as it is more commonly known, is the system of choice for the serious racing sailor. It provides continuous, global, all-weather navigation in three dimensions with high accuracy and great simplicity for the end user. Its accuracy is such that it will go well beyond just telling you where you are. Starting techniques and two boat tuning will change because distances, to the line and between boats, can be measured more accurately than they can be assessed by eye.

So how does this miracle work? The principle is much the same as for Decca and Loran. A receiver aboard the yacht uses timed radio signals to calculate distance from several transmitting beacons. But the position of the beacons is known, and the consequent spherical lines of position are used to triangulate the yacht's position. The biggest difference is that the radio beacons are aboard satellites (see Diagram 1.3). A constellation of 24 satellites in fact, which orbit the earth at a height of 10,900 miles. A minimum of four is visible at any one time, which allows us to calculate position in three dimensions. Trigonometry tells us that each measurement places us on a sphere, and three of them intersecting will place us at two possible points. But one of these solutions will be ridiculous, nowhere near the earth for instance, and so it can be

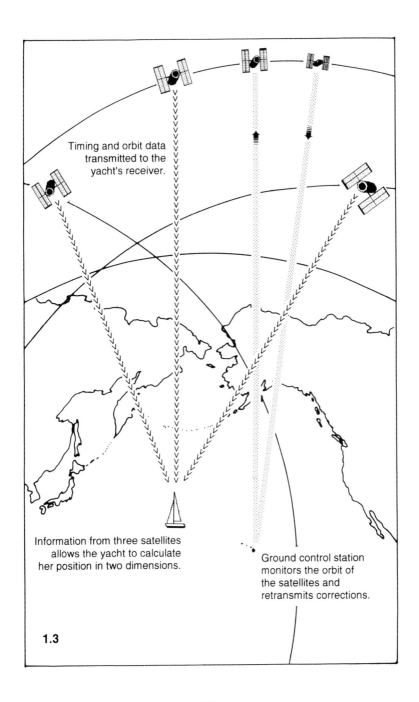

Timing and orbit data transmitted to the yacht's receiver.

Information from three satellites allows the yacht to calculate her position in two dimensions.

Ground control station monitors the orbit of the satellites and retransmits corrections.

1.3

dismissed. The other point will be our position in three dimensions, latitude, longitude and altitude. To see why we need the fourth satellite we must look at how the distance measurements are made.

The distance measurement uses a concept called pseudo-random codes. A pseudo-random code is a succession of noughts and ones apparently at random but which actually repeats itself over a period of time. The satellite transmits these pseudo-random code messages and the receiver listens and compares it to its own internally generated version of the code. All the satellites work on the same two frequencies and they are identified by having their own codes. The underlying assumption is that the code was issued from both sources simultaneously and so by comparing the codes the receiver can calculate the time that the signal took to reach it.

The critical aspect of all this is the timing, because light travels so fast, the tiniest timing error will lead to quite big distance errors. So when we say the codes are issued simultaneously from the satellite and the receiver it must be simultaneous. This requires the most accurate possible clocks on the satellite and the receiver. Putting $100,000 atomic clocks on 24 satellites is one thing, but if every user set required one the potential market would shrink somewhat! The solution is to make an extra distance measurement. We know that the clock error will be consistent to all three measurements. If this is the case then if we introduce an extra measurement the lines of position will not meet at a point (Diagram 1.4). So we tell our receiver that if this happens then it must assume it has a clock error and adjust all its measurements by the same amount until they do meet at a point.

In this way we can eliminate timing errors in the receiver. Timing errors in the atomic clocks aboard the satellites do exist and may occasionally produce a small unknown error in our position even though they are checked and corrected by the ground control system. Of the other errors in the

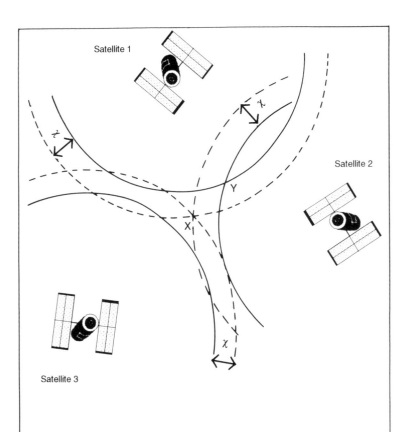

Clock error

Given only satellites 1 and 2, the continuous lines which include the receiver's clock error, meet at point Y. If we then add satellite 3, they no longer all meet. The receiver assumes that this is due to clock error and that the error (χ) is the same for all measurements. It adjusts them by the same amount until they meet at point X - the receiver's clock error corrected position.

1.4

system the worst are probably those due to the ionosphere, which slows down the GPS radio waves an unpredictable amount. We can take account of it using 'average' figures for the effect, but obviously this will never be absolutely right. Although it may not be such a bad solution in the marine case because we only require lat and long, and ionospheric error mainly affects vertical position and time. The atmosphere does have some affect on GPS signals, water vapour will slow and absorb them, and unfortunately it is not an error that we can do much about. One that we can resolve is multipath, the reflection of signals from other surfaces before they reach the receiver - which gives erroneous distance measurements. This can be almost eliminated by continuous tracking of the signal - but it is only something that the more expensive receivers will be likely to do.

Unfortunately the biggest error in the system is put there deliberately. This is selective availability, or S/A, which is the intentional reduction of accuracy of the signals from the satellite by the US Department of Defence. It is done because the system is primarily a military one, and they do not want the opposition using a US navigation system to help shoot at US targets. So the accuracy of the system is downgraded for open use. This is done in two ways; the orbit parameters are offset a tiny bit so that the receiver thinks the satellite is somewhere other than where it really is, secondly the satellite clock is modulated so that the user gets the wrong time. Both these effects are carefully controlled and can be switched on or off. The aim being to give a 100 metre accuracy when S/A is switched on — without it the accuracy can be as good as 20 metres.

When we look at uncertainties in the measurement we must include in our analysis Geometric Dilution of Precision, or GDOP. It effectively magnifies the other errors, by an amount that depends on the angle in the sky the satellites have to the receiver. The wider the angle between the satellites that you are using the bigger the GDOP and the bigger the overall error. The best receivers will look at all the satellites available and choose those that will reduce the GDOP as much as possible — or simply use all of them. GDOP is usually quoted as a single number, you might expect something between two at the best and ten as the outer limit of acceptability.

For the high budget racing programme, such as an *America*'s Cup campaign, there is a solution to all these errors, called Differential GPS. This corrects for them by having an additional ground station in a known position. It can then calculate the error in the GPS position at that point. Because the satellites are so high up this error will be the same in the area around it and the correction can be transmitted to other receivers and used to calculate their positions precisely — and precise means within 2–3 metres. For those that can afford to set up Differential GPS systems, the accuracy opens up a lot of opportunities.

The classic *America*'s Cup programme, as developed by the New Zealanders in 1986–87, with two identical boats testing sails, spars and foils against each other, needs an effective means of working out which boat is the faster. Instrument systems have long struggled with a task they are unequal to, you simply cannot measure performance to the kind of accuracy required to split two boats of race winning speed. The differences are too small — a topic we will return to.

Conventionally, tuning comparison is done in just the same way as you would with a dinghy, you sail the boats beside each other and see who is going faster. But even this is not as simple as it sounds, if the wind heads the leeward boat will seem to get an advantage, if it lifts the windward boat will look good. Whoever is judging the test must not only assess the relative distance and angle of the boats, perhaps using a hand bearing compass or stadiometer, but they must also take account of any wind shifts. It takes practice, and even then requires a great deal of concentration not to make mistakes and come to false conclusions — that might send your whole design programme up the wrong path. But

GPS, a computer and a couple of radios provide an answer. By transmitting the position of the boats to the computer, along with the wind data, it can resolve their distance apart with respect to the wind. At the same time differences in wind strength or direction between the boats can be spotted. Given suitable hardware the computer can record the results of each test run.

The technique was used during the 1987 *America's* Cup with a position fixer called *Syledis*. This is a short range, highly accurate surveying system that was installed in Fremantle especially for the *America's* Cup. Unfortunately, because the whole system, consisting of several radio beacons, required specialists to set it up, it was only available in Fremantle and at the two subsequent 12 Metre World Championships. The simpler and more widely available Differential GPS makes it possible for anyone to use the technique, more or less anywhere. All you need is two boats, radios, Differential GPS beacon, computer and the necessary software (Diagram 1.5). Another possibility is the use of GPS in starting techniques. It would be more accurate to use Differential GPS to call position on a start line than for the bowman to judge it. Again this was used in Fremantle with the *Syledis* system, and is sure to be repeated in the future.

Using the position fixer data
The basic task of a position fixing system is to tell you where you are, traditionally done by displaying a latitude and longitude. This obviously has its uses, placing you on a chart or tidal atlas in relation to the shore, its effects and the tidal streams. But more often you need to know where you are in relation to the next mark. Most position fixers have ways of telling you this, as well as other numbers, but exactly what data you need and how you use it depends on the type of leg you are sailing. What we will look at next is the information you can get from a position fixer, and ways, and ways not, to use it.

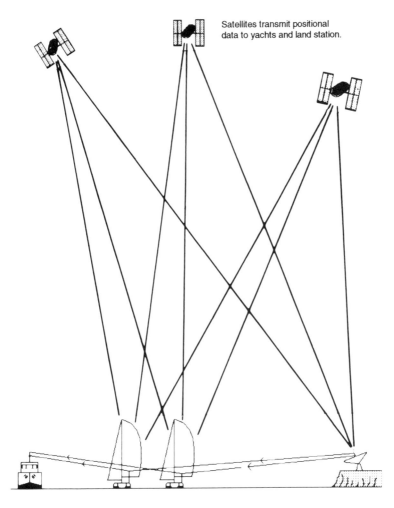

Satellites transmit positional data to yachts and land station.

Position and performance data from both yachts transmitted to tender for analysis.

Position corrections transmitted from differential GPS land station to yachts.

Land station calculates error in satellite position information, because its position is already known precisely.

1.5
Differential GPS in *America*'s Cup Tuning Programmes

COG and SOG; Course and Speed over the Ground
Those of us who race in tidal waters will be familiar with
COG and SOG. If the water is stationary relative to the
ground then your boat speed and heading tell you all you
need to know about your motion relative to the mark. But
if the water is moving, either through tide or wind blown
current, then your course and speed across the ground will
be the vector addition of your boats motion through the
water and the motion of the water relative to the ground
(Diagram 1.6). This is fine if you know exactly what the
water current is, but how often is this the case? It might be
if you have been able to sit by a fixed buoy and measure it,
and you may have a close estimate if you have done the
necessary preparation with a tidal atlas.

It would be far more useful if we could do the calculation

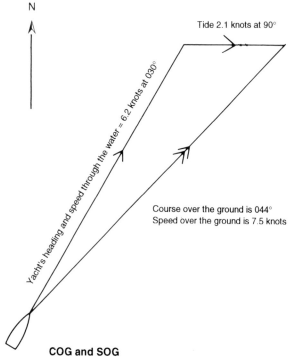

N

Tide 2.1 knots at 90°

Yacht's heading and speed through the water = 6.2 knots at 030°

Course over the ground is 044°
Speed over the ground is 7.5 knots

COG and SOG
The yacht's motion through the water is added to
the water's motion across the ground to give the yacht's
speed and course over the ground.

1.6

the other way around. If we knew course and speed across the ground then we could subtract our boat speed and heading through the water and the result would be the direction and speed of the water flow. This is one use of the COG and SOG figures produced by the position fixer, they allow you to calculate the water flow you are sailing in, and then, hopefully, turn it to your advantage. Some instrument systems, if interfaced to the position fixer, will calculate water current for you. The accuracy with which this can be done depends on how good the position fixer is, in the case of GPS — impressively!

During the 1988 Maxi event in San Francisco Bay, a venue notorious for its strong and unpredictable tides, we were able to use the GPS to stay in the favourable current when, only metres away it was flowing at a couple of knots in the opposite direction. Using COG and SOG to dodge unfavourable tides is straightforward, but tidal strategy gets more subtle.

Take as an example a reaching leg that is sufficiently long for the tide to change significantly, in rate or direction, during the leg. A situation that is different from one where the leg is so short that the tide is more or less constant. In both cases the fastest course is the one which you can sail on a steady compass bearing. Now if the tide is constant the COG will also be a steady bearing, but if the leg is long enough for the tide to change the COG will vary whilst your steering bearing will be the same. Trying to keep the COG the same on a reaching leg with the tide changing is wrong. Whereas with a constant tide, what we are trying to achieve is a heading that will compensate for the effect of the tide and allow us to sail on both a steady steering bearing and a steady COG. The COG should be the direct line across the ground between the marks. The steering bearing can be calculated if you have an estimate of the tide (Diagram 1.7). But in these days of on-deck navigation, or if you do not know the exact strength and rate of the tide, then the COG can be used as a 'cheat'. You just sail the boat at whatever steering bearing gives you the necessary COG to the mark.

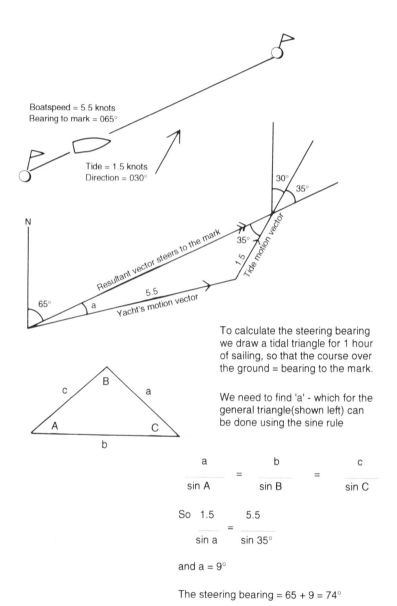

Boatspeed = 5.5 knots
Bearing to mark = 065°

Tide = 1.5 knots
Direction = 030°

30°
35°

N

35°
Tide motion vector
1.5

Resultant vector steers to the mark

65°
a
5.5
Yacht's motion vector

To calculate the steering bearing we draw a tidal triangle for 1 hour of sailing, so that the course over the ground = bearing to the mark.

We need to find 'a' - which for the general triangle(shown left) can be done using the sine rule

$$\frac{a}{\sin A} = \frac{b}{\sin B} = \frac{c}{\sin C}$$

So $\frac{1.5}{\sin a} = \frac{5.5}{\sin 35°}$

and a = 9°

The steering bearing = 65 + 9 = 74°

1.7 Calculation of a steering bearing for a course affected by constant tide

But this technique is disastrous if you try to employ it on a leg where the tide is changing. No sooner have you settled on a steering bearing that gives you the right COG, when the tide changes and you find the COG changing with it. So you correct the steering bearing again to get the COG right and off you go. But as the tide changes the COG will alter once more, and so you will have to change your steering bearing again. This cycle continues with you steering dog-legs across the ocean — not fast at all. What you need to work out is the total amount of tide for the time you are on the leg. Then you can set a course that will compensate for the net effect of the tide over the whole leg. Your calculation will work out from an estimate of your speed and the distance to the mark, how long you will be on the leg. Then, using tidal data you can work out how far you will be pushed off the rhumb line by the tide during each of those hours. Adding them all together you will be left with a net amount of tide pushing you one way or the other — you then calculate a tidal offset to account for just this much tide in the same way as you would for a constant tide. You should be able to sail on the resultant bearing for the whole leg and end up on the mark. Of course, it does not usually work like that, if the wind varies in strength or direction the time you spend on the leg will change, and the tidal estimates are rarely that accurate. So the calculation is one that you must continually repeat as you sail down the leg.

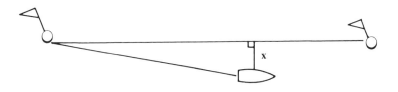

x = Cross Track Error

1.8

But our interest here is in how the instruments can help us sail a leg like this. Which means that it is a good time to introduce Cross Track Error, a position fixer function that can be particularly useful on this type of leg. Cross Track Error is your perpendicular distance from the straight line course between the last waypoint and the one you are sailing to (Diagram 1.8). For the position fixer to be able to calculate this you will need to have programmed in the relevant waypoints. Its use to us here is that it enables you to keep a track of exactly how much you are getting swept off the rhumb line as you sail down the leg (Diagram 1.9). If after two hours you reckoned you would be half a mile south of the rhumb line, and the Cross Track Error only puts you a quarter mile south, then it gives you plenty of time to try and work out what is happening and how to correct it — before you end up a quarter mile south of the buoy and beating back up to it in a foul tide. A move that is unlikely to endear you to any but the most relaxed of skippers.

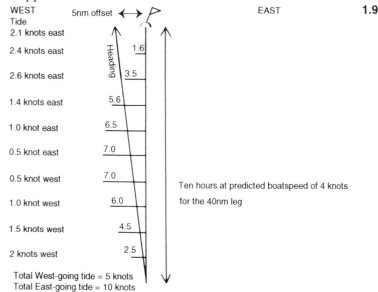

| WEST | | | | EAST | **1.9** |

Tide
2.1 knots east
2.4 knots east
2.6 knots east
1.4 knots east
1.0 knot east
0.5 knot east
0.5 knot west
1.0 knot west
1.5 knots west
2 knots west

5nm offset

Heading
1.6
3.5
5.6
6.5
7.0
7.0
6.0
4.5
2.5

Ten hours at predicted boatspeed of 4 knots
for the 40nm leg

Total West-going tide = 5 knots
Total East-going tide = 10 knots
The total tidal offset for the leg is 5nm West of the buoy. The steering bearing for this is calculated as for a constant tide, by averaging the tidal offset over the ten hours, = 0.5 at 90°. We can calculate our X-track error at the end of each hour (being the tide + 0.5nm West), and this provides a good check on progress towards the buoy.

So much for reaching, the next two position fixer functions we will look at are often of more use on a beat or run. Here, as a navigator you abdicate much of the responsibility, particularly on short courses, for the boats course to the tactician. The COG, SOG and Cross Track Error are not directly relevant to the boats heading, though they still need to be considered. Positional information that the tactician needs to know is the range and bearing of the next mark, and hence your proximity to the two lay lines (Diagram 1.10). Whatever tactical considerations he may have up the beat; wind, tide, shore effects or other boats, he will want to place the boat carefully on the course. Not getting too much to either side too early, and certainly not overstanding. You can use the range and bearing to the mark, together with a knowledge of your COG and SOG to give him this information.

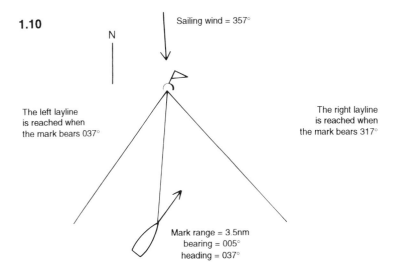

1.10

Sailing wind = 357°

N

The left layline
is reached when
the mark bears 037°

The right layline
is reached when
the mark bears 317°

Mark range = 3.5nm
bearing = 005°
heading = 037°

If you check your heading on each tack you can work out your tacking angle - in this case 80°. Then even if the wind shifts you will know what the mark must bear in order to lay it. If the mark is in your position fixer, checking its bearing will tell you when to tack. When there is tide you can either work out how much to compensate in the normal way, or watch your COG to see how it is affecting you. Your COG on each tack will be the layline bearing - but check the wind, if it alters so will your COG.

There is one important use of COG or Cross Track Error on a windward leg. This example is when you are beating for several hours towards a mark whose bearing lies approximately perpendicular to the tidal stream. In that time you will have several hours of tide running left to right, then several hours of tide running right to left. It is a basic strategy of this type of leg that you set off on the tack which puts the tide under your leebow. I do not want to get into the lee bow effect here, mainly because it would pre-empt what I want to say in the next section, but there is no question that if you have a tide running across a beat, the tack that puts the tide under your lee bow will take you a lot closer to the mark than the one which puts it on the weather bow (Diagram 1.11). The beauty of a long beat where the tide changes half way up is that you can then flop over onto the other tack and so spend the entire time with the tide under your leebow. The advantage of doing this is so great that you would have to have some extraordinarily good reason for not doing it — such as a big, and guaranteed, wind shift!

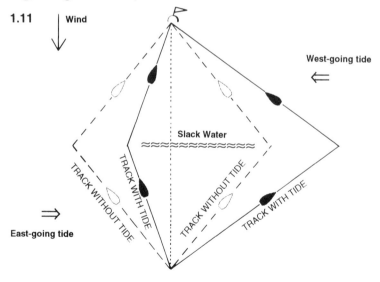

1.11 Wind

West-going tide

Slack Water

TRACK WITHOUT TIDE

TRACK WITH TIDE

TRACK WITHOUT TIDE

TRACK WITH TIDE

East-going tide

Sailing with the tide under the lee bow keeps the boat closer to the rhumb line (and optimises VMC). COG and Cross Track Error can be used to work out when the tide is changing, which is also the time to tack. Other advantages of this technique follow in the next section.

So where does COG and Cross Track Error come into this? Well, the key to it is spotting when the tide has changed and the other tack now has the leebow. Cross Track error will tell you this quickly. When the tide is on the lee bow it will be pushing you up onto the rhumb line, and so the Cross Track Error is a lot smaller than it would be without the tide. As soon as the tide changes the Cross Track Error starts to shoot up as the tide is then taking you away from the rhumb line. The speed with which it increases is your indicator on when to tack. Similarly with COG, it will be steady until the tide goes round, when you see it start to alter, then it is time to go.

Unfortunately we rarely get beats where the wind is steady and the tide changes exactly half way up, and even if we did there may well be some other complicating factors at the next mark, such as a shoreline effect. But what this technique of lee bowing does do is maximise your speed towards the mark — in the jargon, it optimises your VMC. Whether or not this is a good general strategy is something we are going to discuss in the final chapter on instrument techniques using the polar table.

Instrument Systems

Stand-alone equipment versus integrated systems

Yacht instruments can be divided into two types; the first are stand-alone units that provide a single type of data , the second sort is more fittingly called a system — the separate devices being integrated into a whole that is greater than the sum of the parts. Much of what we have to say here is about integrated instrument systems, the reason is that what you get from a stand-alone system is really quite limited. To understand why, let us split up an instrument into its constituent parts. There are three, the sensor that actually measures the physical effect, be it water flow, wind angle or compass heading, the software that translates the electronic blips into a number we can understand, and finally the display unit that communicates this number to the world.

A stand-alone device consists of a single sensor, some software and a display. It is not connected in any way to other devices on the boat, being dedicated solely to the task of telling you one of a limited number of things. This may be either the boat speed, heading, depth, wind speed and angle across the deck, or perhaps the load on various parts of the rig like the headstay. So far so good, all of this information is useful, but not that useful. Instead of just knowing the speed of the wind across the deck, would it not be better if we knew the actual speed of the wind across the water? We cannot measure this, but we can calculate it using the boat speed, and the angle and speed of the wind across the deck.

This is what an integrated instrument system does, it takes the raw data in from all the different sensors and then uses a vector diagram called the Wind Triangle (see next section) to calculate the numbers that will help us race the boat. In addition, because all the numbers are calculated in the same box they can be sent out to any display connected to it. This is quite a lot more powerful, not only do you have more information, but you can display it wherever you want; rather than being locked into just one display for one bit of data as you are with a stand-alone system. For effective race boat instruments an integrated system is really the only choice.

The Wind Triangle and a nomenclature

As we discussed in the section above, an integrated instrument system uses data from several different sensors, then applies some maths to the numbers in order to calculate additional information. The maths involved is known as the Wind Triangle — a vector calculation which we are going to look at here.

The four measurements that are made are: *boat speed*, which comes from some form of impeller, paddle wheel or solid state device and is exactly what it says it is — the speed of the boat moving through the water; *compass heading*, which is straightforward — the magnetic heading of the boat; the final two are the *apparent wind speed* and the *apparent wind angle*, and here we need a definition. The apparent wind is the breeze that you feel blowing across the boat. It is the one that you can measure on-board directly and it is the product of the following three components:

1. The wind blowing across the earth's surface — which we will call the *ground wind*, it is the wind that you will see on the weather maps

2. The wind produced by the motion of the water relative to the land — which we will call the *tide wind*, it is equal in strength and opposite in direction to the water flow

3. The wind produced by the motion of the boat relative to the water — which we will call the motion wind, it is equal in velocity to the boat speed and blows directly onto the bow.

The vector product of all three is the apparent wind, which is the only one of these that we can measure directly. But the Wind Triangle allows us to calculate the others.

Let us assume, for the moment, that we have no position fixer connected into the instruments and that we are out of sight of land, so we have no idea whether or not the water is moving relative to the land. The Wind Triangle uses the boat speed, apparent wind speed and the apparent wind angle to calculate what we shall call the true wind angle and speed — the third side of the triangle (Diagram 2.1). These two numbers are a great deal more useful than the apparent wind speed and angle, for many reasons that will be seen as we continue this book.

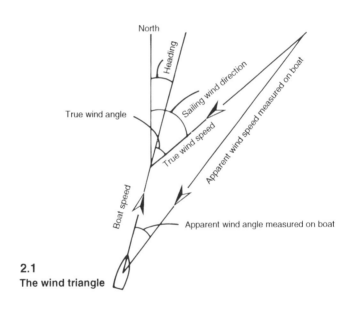

2.1
The wind triangle

The point I want to stress now, is the result of relating this true wind angle that we have just calculated, to the fourth measurement, which is the compass heading. We are presented with what the instruments usually call the *true* or *magnetic wind direction* — and that is probably the most useful tactical tool that you have on the boat, because it is calculated independently of the boat's direction. It is the most precise measure you have of the wind shifts that should be used to sail quickly round the course.

The term I prefer for it is the *sailing wind*; because it is the vector sum of the ground wind and the tide wind and is the wind in which we actually sail (Diagram 2.2). The most important point to grasp here, is that changes in wind speed and direction that you see on the sailing (true/magnetic) wind on the instruments are not just caused by the ground wind altering, they are also affected by the tide changing — because of the tide wind component. The consequences of this fact cannot be underestimated.

2.2

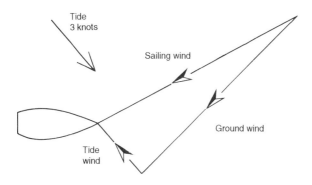

The ground wind and tide wind combine to form the true or sailing wind, whose direction and speed can be calculated from the boat speed, compass, apparent wind speed and angle, as above.

We will start with an example we used a couple of sections ago, when we were talking about a cross-tide beat during which the tide changes. The reason for always being on the tack with the tide under your lee bow, is because this tack is lifted due to the tide wind component. If you were to sail on the other tack, you would be sailing on a header. This header would of course turn into a lift when the tide changes, (Diagram 2.3) which is why you tack when the tide goes round, then on a lee bow tack you are always sailing on the lift in the sailing wind created by the tide.

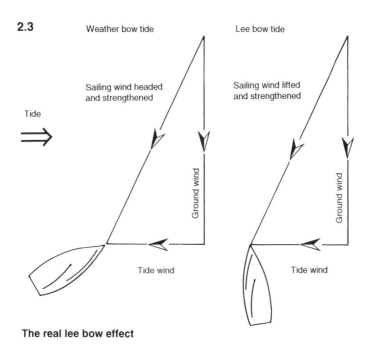

2.3

Weather bow tide

Lee bow tide

Sailing wind headed and strengthened

Sailing wind lifted and strengthened

Tide

Ground wind

Ground wind

Tide wind

Tide wind

The real lee bow effect

The best example I have seen of the dependence of the sailing wind on the tide, happened in the Admiral's Cup summer of 1989 with *Jamarella* (Diagram 2.4). We were sailing upwind beside the Brambles Bank dodging an adverse tide, and as we sailed off the bank and out into the tide on port tack the introduction of the tide wind component caused the sailing wind on the instruments to head by ten degrees. Sure enough the jib lifted and the helm came up as the helmsman accounted for the header. As we sailed back over the bank on starboard and out of the adverse tide we were headed again. This is why it is so important to distinguish between ground and sailing winds — if the wind effect you saw on the last lap was caused by the tide wind, and the tide has now changed, then it is no good going looking for the same effect again. Equally, if you know the tide will change while you are on an upwind or downwind leg, then get on the lifted tack before the tide changes and the lift disappears.

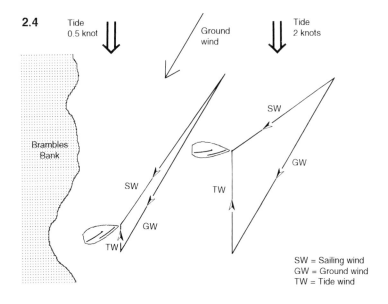

The sailing wind is both headed and drops as you sail into the stronger weather bow tide

Much the same can be said of what is called the true wind speed (a name I am stuck with, as it is uniformly used, along with true wind angle — though needless to say I would prefer sailing wind angle, speed and direction). The true wind speed will go up and down with the tide. If the tide wind is increasing your true (sailing) wind speed, then use it tactically before the tide changes, to cross a patch of rough water for example. To achieve this sort of tactical thinking you will need to know what the tide is doing, so that you can work out the tidal component of the sailing wind you are seeing on your instrument dial. As well as doing the necessary preparation with a chart or tidal atlas you need to watch the tide on buoys and of course the values of COG and SOG as compared to your boat speed and heading; they will also tell you how much of the wind is tidal.

Setting up an Instrument System

Some comments on the calibration process

Three things should be said about the calibration of yacht instruments, firstly, the importance of doing it at all. Any instrument system is only as good as its calibration, you can spend a fortune on the best equipment, but if you do not get out there and set it up properly, you might as well have saved the money. In fact, you are probably worse off than you would be with just a compass on board.

My first experience with instruments was aboard 12 Metres in Fremantle. After a startling promotion from compound-sweeper to navigator, I stepped aboard for the first days sailing. Scarcely had I switched the instruments on, but to find that we were in the middle of a major down-speed tacking duel. By this, I mean that the boat is spun back into the next tack before it has picked up the lost speed from the last one. There seemed to be a lot to do, winding runners, watching lay line proximity and checking the shifts. I decided to concentrate on the wind so that I could at least quickly answer the most obvious question, 'are we up or down?' After five or six tacks I had come to the conclusion that the wind direction I was watching on the dial bore about as much relevance to the wind blowing over the water as it did to the odds of us winning the *America*'s Cup. The result was, that with several tens of thousands of pounds worth of equipment at my disposal, I was completely unable to work out whether we were headed or lifted — not an impressive start.

What slowly became clear was that the wind direction was different on each tack, the size of the error varied with the wind speed, and finally the system was set-up with such a value of damping that in a down speed tack the instruments were not settling to the correct value before we tacked back. All these are things that can be corrected by preparation — so don't skip it.

Secondly, you must approach the calibration in a very systematic order. Everything in the system is interdependent and if you start calibrating in the wrong order you are wasting your time. To see why this is so, we should look at the Wind Triangle that was discussed in the last section. We can see that much of the key information provided by the instruments, such as the sailing wind data, is derived from the measurement of only four values: the boat speed, the compass heading and the apparent wind speed and angle. In fact there is a fifth, the heel angle, but how this is involved we will leave till later. If you start to calibrate one of the functions that is calculated from these numbers, such as the true wind angle, before you have calibrated all of its constituent measured values, like the boat speed; then subsequently calibrating the boat speed will upset all the work you have done on the true wind angle. So the rule is; calibrate every sensor that measures something directly on the boat first, and only when you are completely happy, move onto whatever calibrations are provided for the other functions.

The phrase, 'whatever calibrations are provided for the other functions' brings up an interesting limitation of this book. That it must be written in general terms about something that is specific to the individual reader, ie the instrument system itself. It is a limitation that is going to be most apparent in this section on calibration. Because instrument systems provide the same data, advice on how you use it can be general — but the calibration arrangements are specific. For the values measured by the sensors this is not too much of a problem, the manual will tell you which buttons to press and there are plenty of general points to be made about what you are trying to achieve, and the pitfalls to avoid.

The problem arises most acutely with respect to the functions calculated by the Wind Triangle. Some of you will have systems that provide no calibration facilities for these numbers at all, others will have functions such as mast twist and upwash, or perhaps direct control over the true wind data itself. But ultimately, whatever the system, the problem of calibrating it is the same. My hope is that explaining the problem will help you approach 'whatever calibrations are provided for the other functions' with a clearer view of what you are trying to achieve with them, and how they are supposed to help.

The final point is that calibration is not a one-time task, you never finish the job. The main reason for this is the phenomena of wind sheer and gradient, which we will discuss in the section on apparent wind speed and angle. But don't forget that all the sensors on the boat are mechanical devices that can be moved, bashed, jarred or kicked, from one week to the next. The instruments are never completely above suspicion, but equally when you are confident they are right, you can learn from even the strangest readings — as we will see.

Calibration of the compass

It is always dangerous to generalise, but it's probably safe to say that instrument systems 'generally' use fluxgate compasses. The fluxgate compass measures the field strength around it and so detects the direction of north. This signal is much easier to convert and input into a digital instrument system, than is the direction of the swinging needle of a conventional compass. This has a lot to do with its widespread use in instruments.

Until the late eighties compass calibration was done by a specialist. He would come and tell you, at least on most stripped out racing boats, that you were a degree or two out here and there, and, usually, leave it at that. Technology has intervened, and provided much greater accuracy. The innovation I have in mind is the autoswing facility, which allows the compass, if certain conditions are met, to calculate its own deviation card and then correct the errors out.

The way these compasses work, is to measure the total field strength surrounding them as they turn through a circle. The total field strength measured has two components; one is due to the earth and the other is from the magnetic fields within the boat — all the magnetic sources that create deviation. These two fields are fixed relative to different points of reference. The earth's field is fixed relative to the earth and so the yacht rotates within it. Whereas the deviating fields are fixed to the yacht and therefore rotate with the compass as the yacht turns. Because of this difference the compass is able — using some maths that I couldn't understand, much less explain — to separate them out and so calculate the deviating field. Once it has done this it applies the necessary corrections at all points of the compass.

To make all this happen you usually have to turn the boat in a steady circle, so that the compass can make its measurements, calculations and corrections. This is where the fun starts. The conditions on the turn can be quite stringent, and with *Jamarella* in 1989 we must have tried to do it about four or five times, without ever making a steady enough turn to get the compass to swing. We picked quieter and quieter days, eventually trying in a flat calm, with mirror like water — still no luck.

In this particular instance there was a problem which is worthy of explanation. We had put a cassette speaker on a bulkhead about three feet away from the compass. In theory the compass should have corrected the magnetic field from this in the same way as any other. But it was sufficiently strong to upset the whole routine. There was a particular heading of the boat where the strong field due to the magnet in the speaker attracted the compass. As the boat turned and approached this course the compass heading would tend to rotate faster than the boat, and as the boat turned away from the heading it lagged behind.

This was a problem because the magnetic field of the speaker created a blip in compass heading that fell outside its own parameters of smoothness. So however carefully you steered the boat through the circles the speaker made it impossible for the turn to be smooth enough for the compass to swing. Eventually we moved the speaker, and lo and behold the compass swung at the next attempt. The lesson being that autoswing compasses will autoswing, but only up to a point. The rules about large magnetic fields being placed near them still apply.

Calibration of the boat speed

Boat speed calibration is another job that has been altered by technology — the replacement of the paddle-wheel or impeller by solid state devices. Both paddle-wheels and impellers are mechanical devices that rotate at a frequency proportional to the speed of the water-flow past them. They have a tendency to be erratic, due to mechanical problems such as fouling up and bearing wear, and really need to be calibrated regularly to maintain accuracy. Solid state equipment eliminates this problem because there are no moving parts. *Sonic Speed* made by Brookes & Gatehouse, is an example, measuring the time that sound takes to travel, in both directions, between two points on the hull. The difference is due to the water flowing past the hull and so the boat speed can be calculated. It is more consistent in its measurement than the paddle-wheel, and really only needs calibrating once.

During the 1987 *America's* Cup, the boat speed was re-calibrated once a week on the British 12 Metres. It was an unpopular job, even compared to the alternative early morning physical training routine! *White Crusader* was fitted with both paddle-wheels and a *Sonic Speed* device. During the seven months we sailed her, the *Sonic Speed* never varied, but the paddle-wheels (there were two, one was fitted to each side to eradicate errors due to tacking) almost always calibrated differently. The comforting conclusion is that, once calibrated, the solid state boat speed can be regarded as consistent.

It should be one of the first jobs on any new boat, or at the beginning of the season. If you allow the helmsman and trimmers to get used to one boat speed setting, then decide to re-calibrate, they will find it difficult to adjust to the new readings. So it is important that you calibrate as early, and as accurately, as possible. A comment which holds equally for any type of boat speed sensor. Similarly, whatever the sensor type, the task of boat speed calibration is the same, you need to measure the number of paddle-wheel rotations/sonic blips per knot.

Every instrument system has its own methods for actually doing the calibration, be it just pressing buttons at the beginning and end of each run or using the trusty calculator. Whatever the specific technique required for the instruments, which you will find in the manual, there are some general rules that can be followed to get a more accurate result.

Always steer as straight a line as possible between your chosen distance marks. If it is a proper measured mile then the chart will provide the bearing to steer between the transits. If you have worked out the run yourself then decide on what you are going to steer to and stick to it. If you waver from the straight line then the log will measure extra distance that will not be accounted for in the calibration calculation and this gives you an error.

You should choose a time when the water is flat. The log measures the water flow past it and it is not too choosy whether the flow is created by the boat moving forward or up and down. If the boat is pitching it will record more distance than you have actually travelled. So pick a calm day, and just as importantly a time when there is not too much traffic about. Not only does the pitching from wash affect the calibration, but there is nothing more infuriating than having to alter course from your fixed bearing for someone half way through your final run, so ruining the entire calibration.

Do the runs at fixed engine revs to keep the speed constant. When you turn round at the end of the run the boat will slow down because of the braking effect of the turn. It is important that the turn is sufficiently wide to allow the boat to speed up again by the time you start the next run — otherwise the acceleration will affect the results.

Calibration of the apparent wind speed and angle

Apparent wind speed and angle are measured using a masthead unit that combines anemometer with wind vane. Their calibration problems are connected, which is why we are dealing with them together. Development of the masthead unit has concentrated on reducing the weight and windage, which is particularly critical at the top of the mast and its position in the airflow. It was at the Fremantle *America*'s Cup that they started to sprout in various directions, upwards, outwards, fore and aft, even being moved down to the hounds by the Italia syndicate. The idea behind this is to move the measuring units to a position where they are least affected by aerodynamic errors.

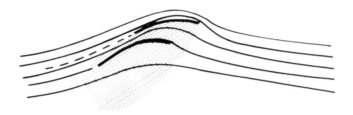

3.1

The sail plan's effect on the apparent wind speed and angle can be seen here

These errors are created by the deflection of the airflow along the sails (Diagram 3.1). This means that the apparent wind is altered from that which is created by the motion of the boat in the sailing wind. The easiest way to understand this is to imagine a motor boat travelling beside a sailing boat at exactly the same speed and angle in a completely uniform wind. If you measured the apparent wind on the motor boat and on the sailing boat, using the instruments on a pole ten feet off the deck, the results would be different. The difference, both in angle and in speed, is due to the deflection of the wind by the sails. Matters can be improved by putting the instruments on top of the mast and raising them as high as possible vertically to get them into clean airflow.

This has the downside that a physical error will be introduced to the angle measurement because the masthead unit twists when the mast tip twists. There is another physical error introduced by the heel of the boat, the angle and speed sensors are measuring the airflow whilst tilted at an angle to it. Although this can be corrected for with a relatively simple calculation, it is probably easier and no less accurate to lump it in with all the other errors involved, and deal with them all together. Having done that, how do we go about correcting them?

For the apparent wind speed and angle there are two ways of approaching the problem. The first, which I favour, is to say that we will ignore these effects and accept the errors as part of the measurement. So we define the apparent wind angle and speed that we measure and use on a sailboat, as including the deflection of that wind by the sailplan. Obviously this makes calibration of these numbers straightforward, but only because it moves the problem down the line to the calibration of the true wind angle and the sailing wind direction. The advantage I believe this approach has, is that the problem is more easily and simply dealt with when you are calibrating the sailing wind. The reason is, that the errors caused by deflection of the wind show up much more readily in the sailing wind, than they do in the apparent wind.

If you had a boat with just apparent wind speed and angle sensors you would never know that the apparent wind was anything other than correct. Your only real comparison point for the apparent wind angle is whether or not it is the same on both tacks, and once you have set this up there is little more that you can do.

With the apparent wind speed there is even less; you have nothing to compare your measurement to — so you simply trust to the manufacturers and leave it. But as soon as you put on board the means of calculating the sailing wind then the defects become obvious. Because the apparent wind is too narrow, or too wide on both tacks, the true wind angle calculated is also too narrow or too wide (Diagram 3.2). Even this would not matter much except that the true wind angle is used with the compass course to calculate the sailing wind direction. If the angles are wider or narrower than they should be, the sailing wind will not meet in the middle — it will be different from tack to tack. Suddenly the defects in your calibration become all too clear.

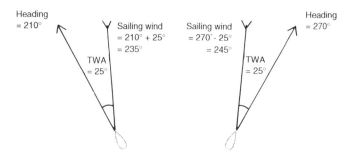

3.2
Errors in the apparent wind angle mean that the true wind angle (TWA) is calculated too narrow. Although the boat tacks through 60°, 2 x TWA = 50°. This means that the calculated sailing wind is backed on starboard tack and veered on port tack from the actual value of 240°.

The second approach accepts this but then goes on to try to calibrate the sailing wind via the calibration of the apparent wind speed and angle. The way it works is that you tack the boat and see whether the sailing wind direction is different from one tack to the other. If it is, then your measurement of the apparent wind speed and angle must be wrong (assuming that the compass and boat speed are calibrated correctly) because the Wind Triangle is coming up with an impossible solution. By adjusting the calibrations of these two numbers you can change their values in the Wind Triangle calculation of the true wind angle. When they are adjusted correctly the true wind angle will give a sailing wind that stays the same on each tack. So you keep tacking the boat, adjusting the apparent wind calibrations and checking the sailing wind direction.

My feeling has always been that this is too difficult, it takes a lot of practice to be able to adjust one number, which only indirectly affects a second, to set up the second number precisely. But because you have no idea what the errors are when you are just looking at the apparent wind angle you cannot calibrate them without using the sailing wind. Which leads us to my preferred solution of leaving the apparent wind as it is. After all it is no less useful because it is a few degrees bigger or smaller than it should be. So why not leave the correction till you get to the true wind angle, where it is important, and it can be calibrated directly and simply? We will have more of this later when we come on to sailing wind calibration.

In the meantime we are left with the relatively simple job of calibrating the apparent wind speed and angle. The apparent wind speed could hardly be easier. Because, as we have already said, there is no possible way of comparing it to any other measurement of the apparent wind speed on the boat, you calibrate it to the manufacturers value and leave it at that. For those with the resources and the inclination the only alternative is to take the unit off the boat and put it in a wind tunnel to check its measurement against a known wind speed. Some of the manufacturers provide this service for their units at a quite reasonable cost.

Unfortunately the matter is not quite so simple for the apparent wind angle, and this is because of another phenomena that we will be hearing a lot more of — wind sheer and gradient. This is due to a law of physics, that moving fluids slow down when they come into contact with the friction of a solid. In this case the air, flowing around the earth as wind, is increasingly slowed as it nears the ground. This is termed wind velocity gradient — the different velocity of wind at different heights. The slowing of air is accompanied by a change in direction, in the Northern Hemisphere the increasing friction backs the wind, ie. rotates its direction anti-clockwise. In the Southern Hemisphere the friction veers the wind, but in all further references to this effect we will assume we are north of the Equator. This effect is called wind sheer

(Diagram 3.3). None of which would be a problem to the instruments if the effect was constant, but of course it is not.

3.3 Wind sheer. In Northern hemisphere wind direction veers with increased height and south of the equator it backs.

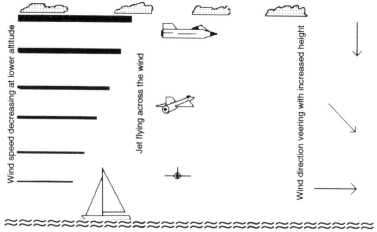

Wind velocity gradient

So how does this effect the apparent wind angle? When we calibrate it, what we are trying to do is get the unit to read zero when it is pointing up the centreline of the boat. So that whether we are on starboard tack or port tack, if the angle we are sailing to the wind is the same then the apparent wind angle reads the same. Wind sheer confuses this considerably — most obviously because the apparent wind angle will not be the same all the way down the mast. The sails will have to be set to some kind of average wind that is utilized over the whole sail plan, and the angle at the top of the mast need not bear any relation to this average sailing angle. Because the wind always backs as it gets nearer the ground what we will see is wider apparent wind angles on starboard than on port, when to all intents and purposes we are sailing at the same apparent wind angle as far as everything else on the boat is concerned.

We can only deal with this by calibrating the apparent

wind angle when there is no, or at least very little, wind sheer. The idea is to leave it fixed at this calibration even when there is wind sheer. Although the numbers seem crazy it is better to know that the instruments are right and that you are looking at a physical effect than to be constantly trying to change the instruments to match a fickle wind. Now we have a Chicken and Egg situation — we need to be able to tell whether or not there is wind sheer so we can calibrate the instruments — without having the instruments to tell us.

The critical factor in the amount of wind sheer and gradient is the vertical mixing of the layers of air. If the air is turbulent then fast moving air from above will be mixed with the ground level wind. There will be little wind sheer or gradient. But if there is little vertical mixing then nothing will stop the lower air from slowing and changing direction. So what causes this mixing? Usually thermal effects, the air near the ground is heated by the land (heated in turn by the sun) and so it rises. Only to cool and drop back down to lower levels. This mechanism mixes up the air. Another method is mechanical turbulence which happens as the air flows across hilly or rough ground. Trees, buildings or mountains, or even rough seas, will all start the air rotating and mixing.

To pick a day to calibrate we need to know the physical signs of these types of mixing. For the thermal case it is relatively easy, cumulus clouds are created by the rising hot air — unmistakeable evidence. With mechanical mixing it is a little more difficult. But any weather system wind that is accompanied by clouds or a frontal system will usually be well mixed. Often because it has been travelling for some time across sea or land. The days you want to avoid are those high pressure days when there is either uniform clouds or clear sky, often accompanied by light winds.

There are other signs you can use as well, associated with the boat. The wind sheer and gradient will make the boat feel different on port tack to starboard. Typically you will be able to sail more quickly on starboard tack, with the sails set with looser top leeches. On port tack speed will be much more difficult to get and the sails will need tight upper leeches (Diagram 3.4). The reason is the change in direction of the wind with height. Because the wind is backing as it gets closer to the ground on starboard the wind angle is wider at the top than it is low down — hence loose upper leeches and plenty of power; whereas on port the top of the sail will be at a wind angle that is actually to tight — hence stalled and low power sails with tight leeches. Look out for these signs and do not calibrate when you see them. Check out the 'Don't Panic' section too, to see how you can make use of this information.

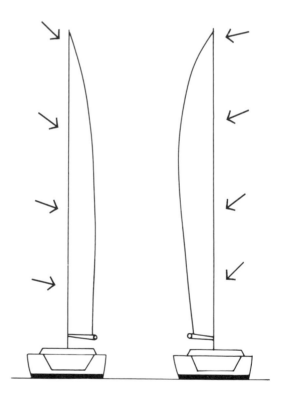

3.4

The effect of wind sheer on sail trim; starboard tack with open top leeches and port tack with tighter top leeches - and vice versa in the Southern hemisphere.

When you have chosen your day to calibrate, the routine is simple enough. First, sail the boat head to wind, having the mainsail up will make it easier to tell when this is the case. The apparent wind angle should read zero, if it does not then reset the calibration so it does. Next, set the boat up on starboard tack so that it feels comfortable. Make a note of the trim of the sails and the boat speed that you are sailing at. Watch the wind angle for a while and take readings so that you can average them out to one apparent wind angle for that tack. Then tack the boat over onto port and set her up in exactly the same way — same trim and the same speed.

The idea is that if these things are equal then you are sailing at the same apparent wind angle. In which case the apparent wind angle reading should be the same as well. Watch it for a while and average the numbers. If you have done the head to wind test properly then they should be close to the same. But the tack to tack test is more accurate, so if the calibration needs adjusting a little bit go ahead and do it (Diagram 3.5). Keep repeating the exercise until you are confident that the apparent wind angle readings are the same on both tacks. Something to watch out for is the sea state, if it is different on the two tacks then even though you are sailing at the same speed you will not be at the same wind angle — take care.

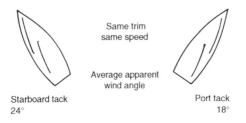

Same trim
same speed

Average apparent
wind angle

Starboard tack
24°

Port tack
18°

Error = 3° on each tack

3.5 Apparent wind angle calibration

Calibration of the depth

The depth is one of the more straightforward calibrations. Partly because it is not connected to any of the other measurements through the Wind Triangle, and partly because there is a fixed measurement to calibrate it to — the depth of water. Having said that the depth can be a rather fuzzy distance if it is a muddy bottom, so try and find a solid seabed to do it on. A lead line is the easiest method, when the boat is in the dock. Measure the depth and then set the datum up so that the depth sounder reading matches it. Depending on whether you prefer to read actual depth or the water under the keel you will need to include the distance from the depth sounder itself to either the bottom of the keel or the water line. Either way you will need to measure this distance while the boat is out of the water. One thing to watch out for is that depth sounders sometimes have trouble getting clear readings in crowded marinas. So if it is reading erratically in any way, wait till you get a calm day and do it whilst you are stopped somewhere outside.

Calibration of the heel angle gauge

Although heel angle does not have a direct impact on the Wind Triangle calculation, it is used in the calculation of leeway (see leeway section). Leeway is used to calculate the course from the compass heading, which some systems may use in the calculation of the sailing wind direction. Even if you are not sure whether this is the case, if your system has heel angle it would pay to calibrate it at the same time as the boat speed, compass and apparent wind, ie. before calibrating the true and sailing wind.

The calibration is straightforward, on a calm day set the boat up with slack warps in the dock and put all the gear in its normal sailing position — including boom and spinnaker pole on the centre-line. Whoever stays on-board should also stand on the centre-line while they read the heel meter. Under these conditions the heel angle should read zero. If it does not then adjust it till it does, either with a software calibration or, if one is not provided, by moving the unit itself.

Calibration of leeway

Leeway is another function, like the true and sailing wind, that is calculated from measured data. The formula used may vary from one instrument system to another. Whatever it is, it will depend on boat speed and heel and should be quoted somewhere in the manual. Let us assume that it is as follows:

L = (K x H) / (BS x BS)

where L   =   Leeway angle
     K   =   Leeway coefficient
     H   =   Heel
    BS   =   Boat speed

The heel angle and the boat speed can be measured directly by the instrument system, the calibration number we need to find is actually the leeway coefficient. There is an easy way and a hard way to do this. The easy way is to ask the yacht's designer the value of the leeway coefficient, the hard way is to try and measure it. Somewhere in the middle lies a short cut which involves taking a guess at it, and then watching the leeway angle calculated by the instruments while you are sailing, checking to see how it matches the design predicted figures. This may not sound very thorough, but the measurement of the leeway coefficient is so difficult that it's probably as good a way as any of doing it.

But if you cannot get any figures from the designer, you can always try and measure the leeway coefficient. The idea being to measure the leeway angle for a particular heel angle and boat speed. Knowing these three numbers you can rearrange the above formula to give you the leeway coefficient, like so:

K = (L x BS x BS) / H

The problem arises when you actually try to measure the leeway angle. This is how it is supposed to work (Diagram

3.6). You pick a day with around ten to fifteen knots of wind, steady in direction, with reasonably flat water. Then sail upwind on a steady bearing recording the boat speed and heel angle as you go. So far so good. You now throw a marker out of the back of the boat. Stand near the mast and using a hand bearing compass take a bearing down the centreline towards the stern. From the same position take a bearing of the marker you dropped overboard. The difference between the two is the leeway angle. This is combined with the boat speed and heel angle that you have been recording to calculate the coefficient. It goes without saying that the flatter the water and the steadier the breeze the easier this is, and even then it is not easy. Personally I have resorted to taking a stab at the coefficient, and then adjusting it so that the leeway angle that the instruments calculate is about 3 degrees when we are sailing upwind in about 10 knots true wind speed and flat water.

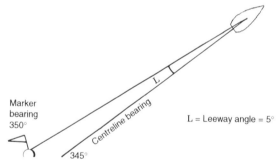

Marker bearing 350°

Centreline bearing

L = Leeway angle = 5°

3.6   345°

Calibration of the true or sailing wind

The calibration of the true or sailing wind is something that we have already discussed within the section on apparent wind calibration. I would certainly recommend that you read that before going any further here. Another section that you should look at is the one on the Wind Triangle. Briefly, what we already know is that the true wind speed and angle and the sailing wind direction are all calculated using the Wind Triangle, and with values from the boat speed, compass, apparent wind speed and angle sensors. Also, once you have calibrated these four sensors your instrument system will work perfectly adequately in every respect except two.

1. The true wind speed will read differently when you are sailing upwind compared to downwind.

2. The sailing wind direction, which is the main tactical tool that the instruments provide you with, will read differently from one tack to the other and from one sailing angle to another.

The reason for this is that the masthead unit is prevented from measuring the apparent wind speed and angle accurately. A couple of factors combine to achieve this, the principal one being the deflection of the wind by the sail plan, but twisting of the masthead unit by the mast is also a factor. So much we already know. We have decided to leave these errors in the measurement of the apparent wind speed and angle, because they are invisible in these numbers. But when the Wind Triangle calculates the true wind speed and angle we know the errors will reappear. Let's take the case of the true wind speed first.

Actual true wind speed = 10 knots

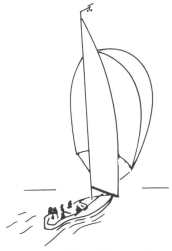

3.7

Upwind instrument true wind speed reading = 10 knots

Downwind instrument true wind speed reading = 11.5 knots

We consistently find that the true wind speed reads higher when you are sailing downwind than when you are sailing upwind (Diagram 3.7). Presumably because the airflow is accelerated past the masthead unit more by the action of the sail downwind, than up. Whatever the reason, the effect is consistent, to correct it you need to take about 15% off the values of the true wind speed that you see downwind. Some systems, instruments and computers, allow you to do this in a table, so that the correction is always made for you. If your instrument system does not have the facility you will have to do the correction yourself each time the boat is about to turn a corner. Note that this error will also exist in the apparent wind. But because the apparent wind is so different upwind compared to downwind it is almost impossible to spot the effect. Nevertheless, if you want an accurate downwind apparent wind speed you should also take 15% off the value on the dial.

The true wind angle is not quite so straightforward. The reason is that the combination of errors that are present at the top of the mast cannot be relied upon to produce a consistent total error. It is dependent on the amount the mast twists, the exact position of the masthead unit and even the sails you put up will have an influence. On some boats the errors will combine to make the apparent wind angle smaller than it should be, on others it will be bigger. Whichever way it goes the error will be carried through into the calculation of the true wind angle. Not that you will tend to notice it here — whether or not the true wind angle is accurate to within 5 or 10 degrees will not be visible when you are using it for trimming or steering. It is when the instruments use it to calculate the sailing wind direction that you will notice the problem. The sailing wind is worked out by adding the true wind angle to the heading if you are on starboard tack, and subtracting it if you are on port. Obviously if the true wind angle is wider or narrower than it should be, then the sailing wind direction will calculate to a different number on each tack (Diagram 3.8).

a) If the true wind angle is too narrow then the calculated sailing wind direction will be backed on starboard tack compared to port.

b) If the true wind angle is too wide then the calculated sailing wind direction will be veered on starboard tack compared to port.

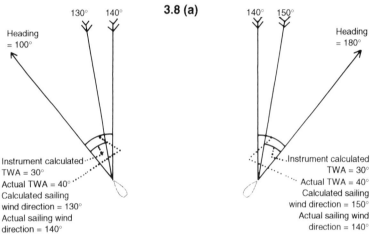

3.8 (a)

When the calculated true wind angle is too narrow - the calculated sailing wind direction is backed on starboard tack and veered on port tack.

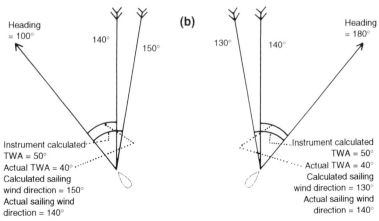

When the calculated true wind angle is too wide - the calculated sailing wind direction is veered on starboard tack and backed on port tack.

A secondary problem exists in that the amount of error in the true wind angle, be it wider or narrower, is not the same upwind to downwind. If you bear away from sailing upwind to reaching, on the same tack, you will find that the calculated sailing wind direction changes even though the wind is steady. We can conclude, firstly, that the true wind angle requires a correction at every point of sailing to make it read an accurate value. We need to develop a table of these corrections, for sailing upwind, reaching and downwind, at each of a band of wind speeds. Secondly, the way to achieve this is by using the errors we see in the sailing wind direction as we manoeuvre the boat, to tell us the corrections we need to make to the true wind angle.

We start by sailing upwind, preferably on a day when the breeze is not too shifty, making a note of the true wind speed and angle, and the sailing wind direction. The boat is then tacked, and after the instruments have settled (see the section on Damping) the new sailing wind direction is recorded. Check that the true wind angle and speed are about the same as they were on the other tack. Then tack back again, and see if the sailing wind goes back to where it was before. You want to be sure that the wind has not shifted while you were tacking, and any difference (or lack of it) in the calculated sailing wind is genuine instrument error and not a wind shift.

Once you are satisfied, work out the correction to the true wind angle required. If the sailing wind direction on port tack is veered compared to starboard, ie 150° on port compared to 130° on starboard, then the true wind angle is too narrow. (It is too wide if the sailing wind direction on starboard is veered compared to that on port). The amount of the correction is found by dividing the difference between the two sailing winds by two, and in the case where the true wind angle is too narrow, adding it on. So in this case we would add:

$$(150 - 130)/2 = 10 \text{ degrees}$$

to the true wind angle to correct it.

Once you are confident of the correction required upwind try sailing along close-hauled then bearing away to a close reach, perhaps a 60 degree true wind angle. Again you should watch the sailing wind direction for any changes, and repeat the exercise several times to be sure that the changes are due to the instruments and not the wind. Assuming that you are on port tack, if, as you bear away, the sailing wind direction veers then the true wind angle at 60 degrees is too narrow compared to the true wind angle upwind. Which means that you must add as a correction the difference between the two sailing wind directions.

Let's take an example (Diagram 3.9), you are sailing along upwind on port tack and the sailing wind direction reads 200°, you bear away to 60 degrees true wind angle and the sailing wind direction changes to 210°. Then we know that we must add the whole of the difference between the two sailing winds, which is 10 degrees, as a correction to the calculated true wind angle at 60 degrees.

Another example (Diagram 3.10), we are now on starboard tack sailing at 120 degrees true wind angle. The wind speed is steady and the sailing wind direction is 300° after it has been corrected upwind. We bear away to 160 degrees true wind angle and the sailing wind alters to 315°. What is the correction required for the 160° sailing angle?

The correction is 15 degrees, the difference between the two sailing wind directions. Now we just need to work out whether it should be added or taken away from the 160° true wind angle. Because we are on starboard and the sailing wind direction veers this means that the true wind angle is being calculated too wide. So we should subtract the 15 degrees to get the right answer. Another way of thinking about it, is to work out what you need to do to the true wind angle, to change 315° to 300°, and the answer must be, for starboard tack, to subtract 15 degrees. Eventually you must slowly and repeatedly manoeuvre the boat through the full range of sailing angles, carefully calculating the necessary corrections to keep the sailing wind direction the same.

3.9

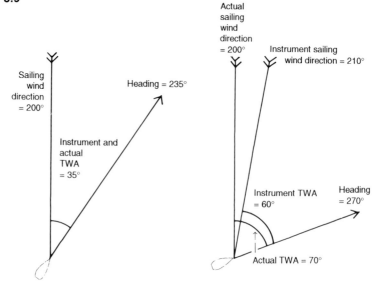

Sailing
wind
direction
= 200°

Heading = 235°

Instrument and
actual
TWA
= 35°

Actual
sailing
wind
direction
= 200°

Instrument sailing
wind direction = 210°

Instrument TWA
= 60°

Heading
= 270°

Actual TWA = 70°

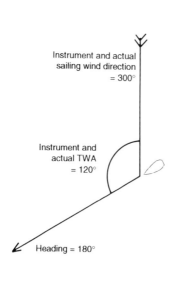

Instrument and actual
sailing wind direction
= 300°

Instrument and
actual TWA
= 120°

Heading = 180°

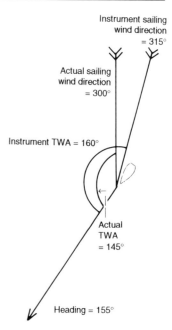

Instrument sailing
wind direction
= 315°

Actual sailing
wind direction
= 300°

Instrument TWA = 160°

Actual
TWA
= 145°

Heading = 155°

3.10

Once you have the table of corrections you should apply them to the true wind angle. Some instrument systems have built in tables that allow you to enter the corrections to them. The instruments then automatically apply the corrections for you depending on the wind speed and angle you are sailing at. Some on board computer systems will do the same job, and it would not be too difficult a task, for the computer literate, to program a lap-top to do it. But failing all that you are stuck with pencil and paper. Even then a correction table, laminated and stuck to the deck somewhere will be remarkably useful.

Take the situation where you are coming into a port round leeward mark, right behind another boat that you are catching fast (Diagram 3.11). You need to know which tack you will be starting the next beat on, in order to decide which side to overtake. Not unnaturally you look at your sailing wind direction to see which tack is favoured, and it says the wind direction is 145 degrees. From your wind readings up the last beat you know that this is a big port tack lift. In which case you would be happy to go round outside him at the mark, so long as you can get clear air, rather than push for an inside overlap.

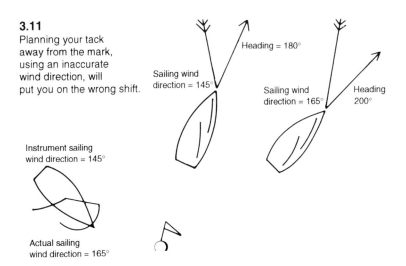

3.11
Planning your tack away from the mark, using an inaccurate wind direction, will put you on the wrong shift.

Sailing wind direction = 145°

Heading = 180°

Sailing wind direction = 165°

Heading 200°

Instrument sailing wind direction = 145°

Actual sailing wind direction = 165°

BUT, your correction table tells you that you should subtract 20 degrees from the true wind angle to get the same sailing wind direction that you had upwind. So you subtract 20 degrees from the true wind angle on port and this veers the sailing wind direction round to 165 degrees. Which puts rather a different complexion on things, now you have a big starboard tack lift. You promptly slow the boat down and round the mark neatly behind the other boat. Now you can tack immediately after the mark and get on that lifted starboard tack. Without your correction table you would have gone round the outside of the other boat, then watched as the sailing wind direction changed to its upwind value and realised you were on the wrong tack. But the other boat is pinning you on port and until you can clear him you are stuck in the header — no way to start a new beat . . . .

One final comment, and this is the bad news. There is absolutely no guarantee that once you have worked out your true wind angle correction table that it will work for more than a few minutes. What!! I hear you cry, understandably aghast that so much work can be so easily destroyed. Well, yes, it can. The conditions of wind sheer and gradient that you do this calibration in seem to have an effect on the results. Quite why this is I can only guess, but you can imagine how a much lighter breeze at water level might be deflected more than a stronger one — and so you need more or less correction for the same wind speed value at the masthead.

The only consolation is that given typical conditions at a particular venue the corrections seem to remain about the same, and when changes do occur they seem to be in size of the correction rather than its direction. So once you have got your table for all the sailing angles it should work most days. Though doing a few tacks before the start to check it out is definitely recommended. But if the weather is unusual or you are sailing at a different venue, ie the Mediterranean rather than the Solent, then expect some different numbers.

Wind sheer has a more obvious effect on the accuracy of

the sailing wind direction. It rotates the numbers by however many degrees of sheer there is. So if you have 20 degrees of wind sheer, which you can see from your apparent wind angle readings, then the wind you are sailing in is up to 20 degrees backed on the wind direction you are reading on the dial. A good way to check this is to work out what the wind should be from your headings on both tacks. If you are sailing at 270°on port tack and 200°on starboard tack then the wind should be blowing from 235°— half-way between the two headings. If the sailing wind dial reads 245°then you have ten degrees of wind sheer. Another way of checking, before the start, is to go head to wind and see if the compass heading, when the boom is flapping on the centreline, is the same as the sailing wind direction.

The main reason you need to watch out for this one is next leg calculations, which we will discuss in the last chapter. But it is fairly evident that if you are using a wind direction that is 20 degrees different from the one you are sailing in, it will throw out any calculations you might do for the next leg. At least it is an easy problem to deal with, just subtract the right number of degrees until the wind sheer goes away.

Don't Panic!
Kiel Week in 1989, British trials for the *Admiral*'s Cup team and the first real racing for the carefully set-up instrument and computer system aboard *Jamarella*. It's half way through one of the inshore races, and, according to the instruments, we were sailing straight into the wind, with an apparent wind angle of zero degrees and a breeze of ten knots. Meanwhile the sails were full and the water was a glassy calm. Confused? Don't be, such apparent instrument anomalies are relatively commonplace — if not always quite as extreme. The crews response is just as common, "There's something wrong with the instruments." (The phrase has a special place in all my worst nightmares). But in this instance there is nothing wrong with the equipment. It is still telling you something, but the message needs more interpretation. Producing good

information when you cannot read the number off the dial directly is one of the key skills of the navigator. So what's the secret?

It is our friends from the apparent wind calibration section — wind sheer and wind gradient. As we said there, with little mixing of the wind aloft and down low there will be big differences in wind speed with height. The type of thing we saw on *Jamarella* that day in Kiel is extreme, but it is perfectly possible that the wind 80 feet up is travelling at ten knots whilst at zero feet it is stationary. Which is what the instruments are telling you. The masthead unit can only measure the wind speed where it is.

This information can be of use to the trimmers, they need to set the sails flat at the bottom, for very light airs, and full at the top for ten knots. At least until you take the wind shear into account. This is allied with velocity gradient, and as we already know, as the wind slows it backs. So that the wind at the masthead is considerably more veered than the wind at the water. Which is why we were able to fill the sails on *Jamarella* even though the wind at the masthead was coming from dead ahead. The wind halfway down the mast was blowing from further to the left (we were on port tack) and filling the sails. Again the instruments were telling all they knew, and the information was certainly of interest to the trimmers. It just needed interpreting correctly. So the next time the trimmer says "There's something wrong with the instruments." Don't panic! Not only are they wrong, but they are the people who need the information most.

Damping — high or low?

Most instrument systems provide some facility for damping the data that they produce. The damping does just what the name suggests — controls the speed of response of the numbers you see on the dial to changes in the raw data. It does it by averaging, over a variable period of time, the data coming from the sensors. The shorter the period of time is, the quicker the values on the dial will respond to changes. This can be advantageous for seeing changes quickly, but you may well find that the numbers jump around so much that it is impossible to tell what they mean. In this case you need a longer damping period to average out all the small, quick changes so that you get a clearer view of the overall picture. Usually there is a happy medium between quick response and smooth changes, but it will vary for different conditions. In big breezes and waves the boat, and therefore the instruments, will be jumping around a lot more and so the numbers will need more damping. In light airs and flat water you can bring the damping right down so that you can pick up the changes in those zephyrs real fast.

If your system only has damping for the sensor values, ie the boat speed, compass, apparent wind speed and angle, then to change the damping of one of the calculated values you may have to change the damping of all the numbers in the calculation. So for true wind angle it would be boat speed and apparent wind speed and angle; for sailing wind direction you will need to change the compass as well. Of course this may mean that these numbers then jump around too much, particularly the boat speed which the helmsman is trying to sail to — in which case you will have to compromise. The time it takes for the sailing wind direction to settle on its new value after a tack is one of the biggest bugbears for the tactician. The calculation of the sailing wind direction involves more components than any other number, and so the damping of all those values accumulate to make it slow to settle. It can easily take a minute after a tack is completed for the sailing wind direction to find its new value. It is important to remember this, reading it too soon will lead to problems whether you are calibrating, just sailing around wind tracking before the start, or on the race course.

Some Instrument Techniques

Start lines and wind shifts

The start of the race will be the first test for your instrument system. You will have two jobs to do, the first being to work out which end of the line has the advantage, and secondly which is the best tack out of the start line. For both of these tasks you will need to use the sailing wind direction. We will leave aside such concerns as general strategy for the course, be it tidal or wind, and any impact this might have on the end of the line or the first tack. The instruments cannot really be expected to help you with this, although we will see later that a computer system can.

Choosing which end of the line to start from means choosing the one closest to the wind. The easiest way to work it out is to take a bearing along the line. Then add 90 degrees if you took the bearing from the starboard end or subtract 90 degrees if the bearing is from the port end (Diagram 4.1). This gives you a value that I call the neutral line wind direction. It is the sailing wind direction that is completely square to the line, ie. there is no advantage to starting at one end or the other. If the wind veers from this then the starboard end will be favoured, and if it backs the port end is favoured. Which means that a glance at the sailing wind direction tells you all you need to know.

So now you just need to track the sailing wind direction down to start time. Using this information you can then pick the end of the line in time to get there for the gun. Remember that if the wind is oscillating you may need to anticipate the shift that you will be on at start time. Imagine a situation where at nine minutes to go the port end is biased, but by six minutes to go the wind has swung and the starboard end now gets the nod. With three minutes to go it is back to the port end — but if you made the decision to head that way you might well find that at the start gun the starboard end is favoured.

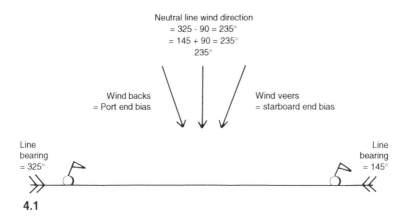

Neutral line wind direction
= 325 - 90 = 235°
= 145 + 90 = 235°
235°

Wind backs
= Port end bias

Wind veers
= starboard end bias

Line
bearing
= 325°

Line
bearing
= 145°

4.1

Tracking these shifts down to start time is more or less just a question of writing down the time and the number on the display. But we must keep in mind all we have said in the previous sections about calibration and damping. You must check the calibration of the sailing wind before you start taking wind readings. Calibration errors are often particularly severe when you are tacking reach to reach — which tends to happen quite a lot before the start. Don't be fooled into thinking that there are huge shifts around when there are not. Damping is another problem when the boat is being thrown around in the starting area. Particularly when it is combined with lots of dirty wind from all the sails and confused seas. In fact when it comes down to it you will be hard pushed to get a decent reading when you get into the final approach to the line. So it is really important that you have a clear idea of what wind directions you are expecting to see once you clear the line.

The start is a time when you must try to divorce yourself from everyone else's immediate concern — which is getting a good start — and look ahead to the first couple of minutes of the beat. Your first job is to work out what the wind is doing as you come off the line. Which means you have to know whether the instruments are settled on the number they are showing, or just spinning past it as the damping tries to cope with some radical manoeuvre the boat has just done. In short, you need to watch it all the time. It is never easy to ignore the excitement of a start, but you look pretty average when as soon as you are off the line the tactician turns round and says 'Are we up or down?' and you do not know.

One complication you need not worry about is the effect of the tide on the start line wind. Sometimes an inexperienced race officer will set a badly biased line. The reason for this is that he is measuring the wind direction from a boat that is anchored to the seabed — and so it is the ground wind that he is recording. You are sailing in water that may be moving relative to the seabed and so your sailing wind will have a tide wind component, as we mentioned in the section on the Wind Triangle. This tide wind component can alter the wind you are sailing in quite dramatically (Diagram 4.2). So if you ignore the tide and set the line to the ground wind you may well have a substantial bias. The good news is that your on board instruments, so long as you are sailing and not anchored, will read the sailing wind that includes the tidal component. It is only the race officer, who is anchored, that must account for it in his calculations.

4.2

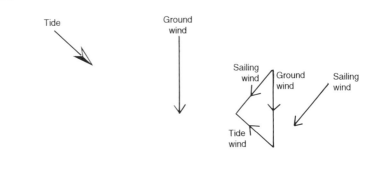

This line would be square to the ground wind, measured from an anchored committee boat, but has substantial starboard bias to the tidally altered sailing wind.

One final point about wind shift tracking. We had mentioned earlier that changes in wind gradient and sheer may effect the calibration of the sailing wind direction. Which poses a problem, how are you supposed to recognise calibration that has altered whilst you are racing? If, for instance, it started altering when you tacked, in a manner that your calibration did not account for, how would you know? Would you not just assume that the wind was shifting as you tacked? For a while you might, but after three or four times you ought to be suspicious. But three or four tacks on dud information could cost you the race, so here is a check you can use. Keep a note of your compass headings on each tack as a back-up. These will also tell you if you are headed or lifted, so as soon as you are worried that the sailing wind direction is playing up you can check what it is telling you against the heading.

Unfortunately there is a problem with this as well, since the true wind angle a yacht sails at is dependent on the wind strength. The more breeze there is, the closer you can sail to the wind, until about fifteen or twenty knots when the angle does not get any narrower, and may even widen as the wind increases towards thirty knots. So your compass will often tell you that you are headed or lifted when in fact the wind direction is the same but the wind velocity has altered. This is known as a velocity header or lift, and is accentuated by what happens to your apparent wind when the sailing wind first changes.

Diagram 4.3 shows the case of a velocity header. As the wind drops, the boat has sufficient momentum to keep its speed for a few seconds, which moves the apparent wind forward, lifts the jib and gives the impression that you have been headed. It is important that the helmsman does not bear away too hard when this happens, because as the boat slows down to match the new windspeed the jib will stop backing, and you can gain ground to windward by holding course and letting the speed drop until the jib refills. You will have to bear away a little because of the new wider true wind angle for the lower windspeed.

Do not be fooled by the velocity header into tacking, and equally important; be careful when checking your sailing wind direction against the compass heading, that you do not start worrying about the sailing wind direction unnecessarily. The sailing wind will ignore velocity headers and lifts, whereas the compass will not. So you really have to keep an eye on them both, each to check the other. In the next section we will see how we can use the heel angle to help with a similar problem with the true wind speed.

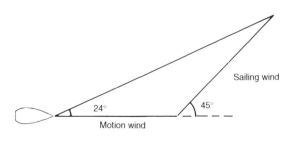

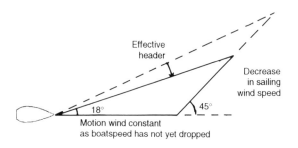

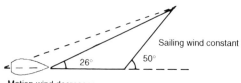

4.3

Heel angle or wind speed?

In the *Don't Panic* section we looked at an example, albeit extreme, where the wind speed read ten knots at the top of the mast, and the water was a glassy calm. The effect of wind sheer and gradient meant the instruments required careful interpretation. We looked at how to deal with the apparent wind angle, but not the wind speed, which you do need for sail selection and target speeds. So what do you do when the wind is seriously mixed up about its strength? The answer is to use the heel angle.

At any sailing angle, other than downwind, the heel can be an excellent measure of how much pressure there is in the wind. This is what you are using the wind speed to tell you, so that you can match your sails to the wind pressure available. Under average conditions of wind gradient it is a reasonably good guide. But it will always be limited by the fact that it is only measuring the wind speed in one place. And the wind is quite capable, and equally likely, to change at a height other than masthead. In this case the only way you will pick up the change in available wind pressure on the instruments, is with the heel angle (Diagram 4.4).

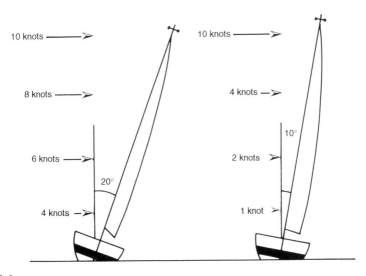

4.4

Before I go any further I should put in a proviso. The heel angle is not only dependent on the wind speed. Sail choice, trim, steering technique etc. etc. will all effect it as well. But when you are sailing along in a straight line and all these things are more or less constant, and then suddenly the heel angle starts dropping with the wind speed steady, it is clear what is happening.

I have seen this type of thing most often in the Mediterranean, which is prone to the light and fickle conditions where the technique is useful. It is in places where the wind gradient comes and goes, or bands of warmer air blow in (which is less dense and therefore exerts less pressure), that the wind speed measurement becomes less trustworthy.

Keeping an eye on the heel angle can give you that vital first clue to what is going on. But do not expect the technique to work when you are crashing upwind in twenty knots, the heel angle will be jumping around far too much to be useful, unless your instrument system has the facility to dampen it. Fortunately in these conditions the wind is usually steady and consistent at all heights and the wind speed does the job it was intended for perfectly well.

Anticipation

Anticipation is not so much an instrument technique as a state of mind. Because of the greater emphasis on tactics in short course racing, you will spend less time working on strategy and more supporting the tactician with the information he needs for his decisions. The key to doing the navigator's job well is to anticipate what the tactician is going to want to know next, and start working it out before he asks for it. There are endless possible examples — as many as there are tactical situations. I have pointed out a couple below. If there was one single piece of advice I would give to a big boat navigator on this subject, it is to do some small boat racing as a helmsman and decision maker. There is no faster way to get an insight into what information the tactician is likely to require. Then read all the books on yacht racing tactics and also those on navigation.

The first example comes up all the time. On port tack, heading towards the starboard tack lay line and apparently on a collision course with two yachts on starboard tack, the tactician needs to know whether or not those boats are laying the mark before you get to them. He has to decide whether to duck behind them or tack underneath. If they are laying the mark comfortably then a tack to leeward and slightly ahead will see you round in front. If they are not laying it would be preferable for you to duck behind them and sail on to the lay line. The navigator should see this coming way before it arrives, particularly in a tidal situation where it is much harder to judge the lay line by eye.

The second example occurred during the final inshore of the 1989 *Admiral*'s Cup, aboard *Jamarella*. A backing shift had come in on the first beat and we were sailing to the gybe mark on a tight reach, fourth of the Fifty Footers. The last of the leading three peeled round and gybed, when we were about fifty yards from the mark. The tactician asked if we could carry on, meaning had the wind swung enough to make the next leg a run rather than a reach. If it was a run we could start it on either gybe, but preferably the one that was most advantaged by the present wind shift. I had been looking at the problem for a minute or so, it was certainly a run, the question was whether or not starboard put us on the best shift. By the time the question came I was able to answer yes. The gybe was cancelled and we squared away on starboard. A couple of minutes went by and the breeze lifted us, which downwind takes you away from the mark. So we gybed, and now laying the mark on the paying tack, ran down to it and into 2nd place.

The wind shift coming through when it did made us look particularly smart — but starting to look at the question before it was asked was the only way to have the answer ready in time. A good tactician will expect this sort of anticipation, it is not his job to be warning you of every possible situation that might arise. He is going to ask the question when he needs the answer, which is usually immediately. So keep your eyes on the race course, concentrate and anticipate.

Polar Tables
and where they come from

What are Polar Tables?

All of the instrument techniques that we have looked at so far have used either position on the race course, or the Wind Triangle and the resultant numbers that we can calculate from it. There is a third branch of information that is just as important to the navigator — performance data. Although it is not immediately obvious why this should be of interest to the navigator, we will see that it has both tactical and strategic uses — as well as improving the speed of the boat. The whole topic of yacht performance and data analysis centres on the polar table.

The polar table gives us a convenient way of recording performance, both graphically and in a table. It takes each wind speed separately and for every true wind angle records the boat speed of the yacht. These are then plotted on a polar diagram using one line for each wind speed, the angle from the vertical representing the true wind angle and the distance from the centre representing the boat speed (Diagram 5.1).

Polar Table accuracy

Now we know what polar tables are, we can go on to look at their derivation and use — the topics of the rest of this, and the next chapter. But the usefulness of the polar table is dependent on its accuracy, something we should discuss first. In a sense we are going over old ground, since many of the reasons for polar table errors have already been come across in the chapter on calibration. Obviously, calibrating the system carefully will eliminate as much error as possible. However, there is one major difficulty that limits all our efforts, which at the moment cannot be resolved. That is the problem of wind sheer and gradient.

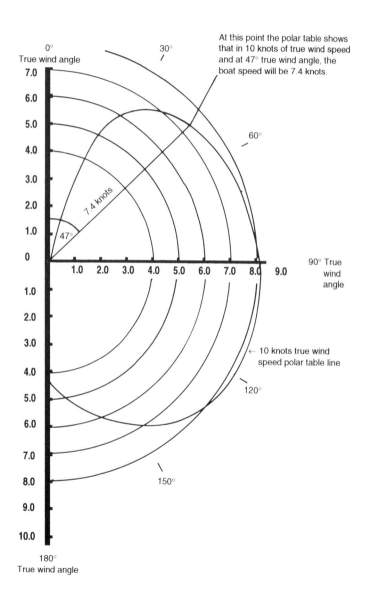

5.1 The polar table

We have already established that the polar table measures the boat speed at each particular wind speed and angle. Each point on the table represents the balancing of the water and wind forces on the yacht. The wind speed and angle are measures of the aerodynamic force available, and the boat speed measures the hulls equal and opposite hydrodynamic response.

Measuring the speed of the boat is fine, so is measuring the true wind angle, if it is defined as half of the angle that the boat tacks through. But we cannot measure the true wind speed, as it relates to boat speed. We can measure it at the top of the mast, but if we try to use this number as the pressure that the wind is supplying to drive the boat forwards, we will fail. The reason is, that the wind can have any value below the masthead, whilst the masthead value stays the same. We could read ten knots at the masthead and be reaching at a cheerful 6 knots, with a breeze that was ten knots virtually down to the water. Alternatively, we could be sitting becalmed, still recording ten knots at the masthead but with a breeze that stubbornly refused to come any closer to the sails. How is any polar table based on masthead values of wind speed going to cope with that? The answer is — not at all. And until we find a significantly better way of measuring the wind power available to the rig and build our polar tables around it, their usefulness will be limited.

That's the bad news. The good news is that in practice, if you sail at the same venue, in roughly the same weather conditions, be they sea breezes or frontal systems, then the wind velocity gradient will not change that much. You can use your polar table — otherwise I would not have devoted some considerable space in this book telling you how to do so. But never consider it cast in stone. As soon as you get a different weather type, or sail somewhere new (like move from the Solent to the Mediterranean) you can expect problems. Approach polar tables with a healthy scepticism — that's the rule.

Velocity prediction programs

Velocity prediction programs, or VPPs as they are known, are computer predictions of a yacht's performance. The computer has a model of the design in its memory, which the VPP then analyses to calculate how fast it thinks the yacht will go at different true wind angles and speeds. It does this by calculating the amount of drag the yacht will develop to stop it accelerating and the amount of drive the rig will generate to push it forward. It then uses the inherent symmetry of sailing to predict the boat speed at which these two factors will cancel out. Where the aerodynamic driving force is exactly matched by the hydrodynamic drag, the boat speed is the best that can be achieved for that wind speed and angle. The most obvious use of something like this is in the design process, where VPPs can be used to test and refine designs before they are ever built.

Another use has been developed with the IMS rating rule. This system machine measures the hull and rig once they are built and, after entering the hull lines into a computer, uses a VPP to predict the performance. The rating is then based on the performance profile. The big advantage of this over a traditional rating system, like the IOR, is that the boat can be rated differently through a range of conditions to allow for its particular characteristics. So light air flyers get a rating that means they have to fly in light air to win, but equally, it does not penalise them for their performance when the breeze is up and makes it impossible for them to sail to their optimum speed.

This rule, more than anything else, has made VPPs accessible to a wide number of yacht owners. Anyone with an IMS certificate now has access to a VPP analysis of their boat. As do the owners of custom or one-design yachts where the designer has used a VPP in the design process and makes it available. Our interest is whether the polar tables generated by the VPPs can be used for the tactical and performance analysis techniques that occupy the rest of this book. And the answer is a conditional yes. Whilst VPPs are not perfect, they do seem to be an effective design tool in that they can usually compare designs and differentiate the one that will be faster in both the real world as well as the computer world. But this does not mean that the actual performance numbers predicted can be directly lifted onto the yacht.

The reason being that the measurement of the yacht's real performance, whilst it may be consistent with itself, is unlikely to be accurate in an absolute sense — which is what the VPP requires. Just one aspect of this is the way your boat speed calibration varies with heel angle. The boat speed sensors are measuring the water flow under the hull, which is a function of the boat speed rather than the boat speed itself. If this function alters with the heel angle then you should have a different calibration for the boat heeled as opposed to upright. Of course we do not, and this means that whilst the boat speed reading is consistent on the boat, it will vary when compared to an absolute measurement; ie. for an identical hull speed through the water, the boat speed might read 8 knots going downwind and 7.8 upwind, because the water flows past the boat speed sensor differently when the boat is heeled to when it is upright. But because it always reads 7.8 when you are going upwind at that hull speed, the instruments are always consistent with themselves, and it is not a problem when you are sailing. It becomes one when you try to compare your measured figures to VPP figures which have no allowance for the practicalities of your instrument system.

A bigger problem, as usual, is due to our rather tiresome friends, wind sheer and gradient. For the VPP to match your sailing numbers on the water, you need an equivalent wind gradient to that assumed by the program, and also the wind speed measured at the same height. The chances of this happening are slim — there are bound to be differences. But the differences produced by these problems tend to be in the magnitude rather than in the shape of the polar curves. This means that the VPP figures for a given wind speed will produce a polar curve of the same proportions as the real data — although all the boat speeds may be either a little higher or a little lower. At least in my more recent experience, this has been the case, and we can expect the VPPs to get better all the time. It means that your VPP polar is a good enough place to start the generation of the yacht's polar table. You will certainly have to correct it, but it is likely that the corrections will be of a similar amount and type for much of the table. So if you can get hold of a VPP for the boat, use it as a start point for performance analysis. But I would not recommend too much reliance on it for exact target boat speeds or tactical techniques until you have had a good opportunity to test it.

Velocity made good and target boat speeds

Before we move on to performance analysis there are a couple of concepts that we need to introduce. The first is velocity made good or Vmg, which is defined as the boat speed multiplied by the cosine of the true wind angle (Diagram 5.2). It is a measure of how efficiently you are sailing to windward — it increases if you can sail either closer to the wind at the same speed, or at the same angle to the wind but faster. We are usually interested in two particular values — the maximum Vmg that can be achieved upwind, and downwind. These are both numbers that we can find using the polar table.

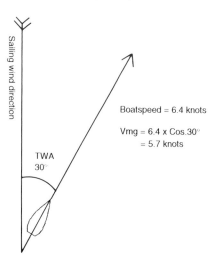

Sailing wind direction

Boatspeed = 6.4 knots

Vmg = 6.4 x Cos.30°
= 5.7 knots

TWA
30°

5.2

82

Referring to Diagram 5.3, we take a horizontal line, perpendicular to the zero true wind angle line, and lower it until it touches the top of the polar table. Then the maximum upwind value of Vmg is given by the vertical height up the zero true wind angle line, using the same scale that the boat speed is plotted on. The same principle is followed for the downwind Vmg. Equally important, is that the boat speed and true wind angle that give the optimum Vmg can be read off the polar where the line touches. This speed and angle are known as the target boat speed and target true wind angle for upwind sailing. They are target values because they are the values we must try to sail at to achieve maximum performance upwind. The target values for downwind sailing are obtained in the same way.

The question of why you are sailing to a target boat speed when it is the Vmg that you are trying to optimise needs to be answered. The problem with Vmg is the momentum of the boat. If you sail watching the Vmg you will see that the closer to the wind you go the higher the Vmg gets. This is because the true wind angle is getting narrower, but for no corresponding loss of boat speed. The boat is maintaining speed because of its momentum. So you keep steering closer to the wind and the Vmg keeps getting higher. Until finally the boat runs out of steam and the boat speed comes crashing down, taking the Vmg with it. It is this lag in the response of Vmg to your sailing angle that has led to the technique of sailing at the boat speed which is known to optimise your Vmg.

This is best achieved by programming your instruments to display on a dial the target boat speed for the wind speed it is measuring. Since the target varies as the wind speed goes up and down, having the polar table in the instrument system so that it can update the value for you is a big help to the helmsman. Downwind it is sometimes easier to sail the boat at the true wind angle that matches the target boat speed, rather than aim for the boat speed itself. On a free leg where there is no need to tack, the principle is even simpler. Using the true wind angle that you are sailing at

5.3 Velocity made good and target boat speeds

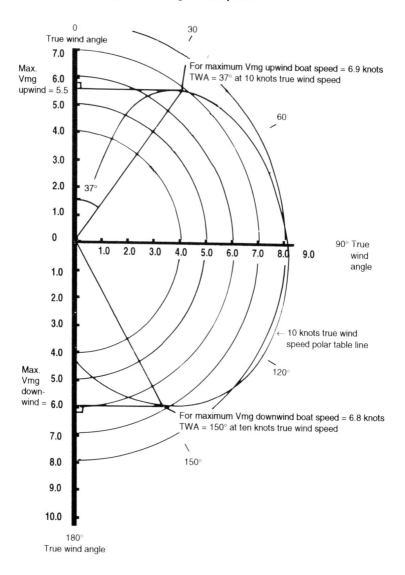

to make the next mark, you look up in the polar table the speed you should be achieving at that angle and wind speed. This is your target boat speed for the leg.

We must finish with the familiar proviso that all this is dependent on the polar table which is variable according to the wind gradient. So do not set too much store by your targets. If you can beat them easily, do not relax, revise the targets upwards. It is for this reason that I have never really approved of displaying targets for free legs. The best means of sailing the boat at its optimum is simply to race hard against the boats around you. But when you are offshore on your own, or at night, they can certainly help. For Vmg legs their usefulness is well established. The helmsman is better off with something to aim at, though he may well be revising the number he sees against what he feels from the boat. It is not unusual to be deliberately sailing two or three tenths above or below your target because of the particular conditions. The helmsman's feel, if he is any good, is a lot more sensitive than your instruments. If he is not, you are probably wasting your time anyway!

Data collection and performance analysis

This is a topic that I feel a little unqualified to tackle. A Ph.d in statistics would just about get me there, and then I think you would need a whole book to do the subject justice. Having made that disclaimer I am going to restrict my comments to the practical experience I have had trying to optimise and record yacht performance. Firstly, you should read the section on 'Polar Table Accuracy', where we discussed the limitations imposed on the use of data collection and analysis to improve performance. The problem is, that you cannot know whether or not the wind conditions are actually the same as the last time you collected the data, even though the instruments say they are.

One consequence of this is that the polar table itself is only an approximate record of the yacht's performance. It is possible for polar figures that you collect one day to be a knot out the next day — purely due to changes in wind gradient. So the idea of testing your boat against a continually updated polar table in a computer is a non-starter. With it goes any hope of testing one mast or keel configuration against another. In the time it would take you to change those items, all certainty that the breeze was the same would be lost. You cannot run the results of a test done one day against results from a different day.

You can however, test items that can be changed quickly — such as sails or trim. What you are aiming to achieve, is to make direct comparisons on the day, establishing facts such as one genoa's superiority over another in a particular wind speed, type of wind and sea state. You cannot record the Vmg or speed achieved with the sail in those conditions, and then test another sail against those numbers on another day. You must do a comparative test on the same day, as close as possible to get any meaningful results.

We need to distinguish two separate jobs. The first is the production of a general polar table that we can use, despite its problems with accuracy, to sail the boat tactically as well as giving rough performance guides. The second task is testing different configurations of the yacht; sails, trimming and so on, by a comparative testing technique.

When generating the polar table or for comparative testing, you will need the facility to collect and average the instrument data. This can be done with a pen and paper but it is much better to use a computer. If you do not have access to some kind of portable machine that you can put aboard the boat, then your energies would be better directed elsewhere.

Most instrument systems have a data output on what is called an RS232 serial link. Any computer with an RS232 port can be programmed to receive this data and average it over a period of time. If you do not have the computer skills necessary to achieve this, the best people to talk to are usually the instrument manufacturers. If they cannot help they will put you in touch with someone who can. There is proprietary software available for this job, but it can often be done just as effectively with a spreadsheet program. You load the numbers in columns into the spreadsheet, then take averages over the necessary time periods that you were sailing or testing.

I would suggest, quite strongly, that you do all this work on the water. You can put the lap-top down below if you do not have a waterproof system. The reason for doing it in, as the jargon has it, 'real-time', is that you are much more aware of the variables that the machine cannot record. The wind gradient is one that we have discussed ad nauseam, but variations are also due to sea state. If you do your data averaging and analysis at the time you will know that you spent four minutes of that test wallowing in the wake of a tanker, and either bin the test or cut those figures out. You cannot see that afterwards, unless you keep comprehensive notes. So the basic testing set-up is a lap-top computer, either on-deck or down below, connected to the instrument system via the RS232 port. It's running a spreadsheet, or some similar software package, into which the data is streamed, so that you can calculate average figures for each of the values you are testing as quickly and easily as possible — preferably during sailing.

Assuming that you have managed to arrange this, how do you go about generating your polar table? There are two ways of doing it, one is to deliberately sail the boat to requirements, the other is to try and pick up data whilst the boat is sailed around at the behest of the rest of the crew. Which of these you choose depends on how much time you have on the water. If your boat only goes sailing to race then you will have to do the analysis from data gathered while you are racing. In which case it is difficult to devote yourself to the task at the time, you will almost certainly be forced back onto post-race analysis of data. The best way to salvage this situation is to keep as detailed notes — when the boat was going well, badly, when the data was messed up by some unusual circumstance and so on.

It is more efficient to control the situation and do the analysis whilst you are sailing. Either way you are looking for the same thing; periods of sailing at about the same true wind angle and a reasonably consistent wind speed. How you find these, depends on what set-up you have — some spreadsheets will graph the data and allow you to check it for consistency easily. Without that facility you will have to look at the numbers themselves. Once you have found a likely looking set of data it is a matter of finding the average of the values involved; the true wind speed, angle and the boat speed. If you wanted to be really thorough you might set parameters for the figures, such as a minimum time limit on the set of data and standard deviation limits that they must better. In this way you build up your collection of polar points, adding each one to the table as you go along.

The job will be a lot easier if you have some figures to start with. However rough an approximation they may be, it will at least give you a whole set of data that you can refine as you go along, rather than starting with a blank sheet of paper. This is where a VPP can be particularly useful as a start point. The thing about polar tables is not to get too concerned about accuracy. There are such big problems with them anyway that anything close to the rough shape will do a decent job for you. Plus or minus five percent, which would be a respectable error, gives you a one knot error range at ten knots boat speed. So don't get too psyched up about pinning down those hundredths of a knot you see on the dial.

Whilst you need not worry overly about accuracy with the polar tables, comparative testing is a different ball game. Two boats sailing beside each other for ten minutes at six knots, with one pulling out a twenty foot gain represents a significant winning margin. That twenty foot gain represents a two hundredths of a knot speed advantage, the margin between winning and losing, and the magnitude of advantage that you would like to spot. Which only goes to reinforce what we said earlier about polar tables not being capable of recording results that you can tune against in any worthwhile sense.

Although the margins that you are looking at are tiny, it is still possible to make performance distinctions, if not quite that small, then close to it. But you need the absolute cooperation of the crew, and reasonable cooperation from the wind. There is no question here about doing it under normal sailing conditions followed by post analysis of the data. The one consolation is that you can at least use the data generated from testing in your polar table as well. You must sail the boat for ten or fifteen minutes at a time in each of the different modes that you wish to test. For each test you record the boat speed, Vmg and the true wind angle and speed. At the end of the test you can average these numbers and record them for that sail. Some limits must be placed on the variation in the wind speed, otherwise the data will have such a wide spread that you cannot rationalize anything.

Once you have your averages, set the boat up for the second test and sail again. Try to keep the boat sailing in as similar a fashion as possible to the previous test. If you sail it at the same boat speed then a drop or improvement in performance will show up through the true wind angle and Vmg. Of course you cannot control the wind, and it is frustrating how many of these tests have to be aborted because of changes in wind speed.

If statistics is your forte, then you might try adjusting all the Vmg and true wind angle values to the average wind speed. A process which, whilst not for the statistically faint-hearted, does make the testing a lot more productive. But in theory you should be able to choose a winner from each test. Then you must repeat it, going back to the earlier set-up and doing it again. You may or may not get the same winner, and you keep going until it is clear which is the superior sail — or that the difference is so small you cannot distinguish it. Do not kid yourself about this job, it's a major task.

There is one other problem that people like to tackle with these techniques, and that is finding the target boat speed. We have already said that this is the boat speed that we sail at to achieve the optimum Vmg, either to windward or downwind, and we have seen how it can be derived from the polar table. It is an obvious application of our comparative testing techniques to try and find this target boat speed.

It may seem that you should be able to let the helmsman sail the boat at its best, for twenty minutes or so in a steady breeze. The natural ups and downs of steering the boat will give you a nice spread of data. You can then plot out the polar table line for whatever wind speed you were testing at, as we looked at earlier, and derive the target boat speed. It is actually easier to plot out the boat speed and the true wind angle separately against the Vmg. The result ought to be an inverted U that peaks nicely at the boat speed and the wind angle where the maximum Vmg is obtained (Diagram 5.4).

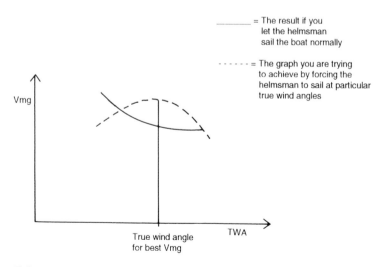

5.4

It does not work like that. What seems to happen is that the helmsman's steering technique exploits the wave pattern so that he gains ground to windward every time he gets a chance to do it, but without letting the boat lose any speed. This seems to give you a whole load of numbers at narrow wind angles and average boat speeds with consequentially high Vmgs. The result of the above test is almost invariably a graph that shows Vmg increasing the higher you sail. Of course if you actually do this you end up head to wind and stopped dead. It seems that the aspect of the test that the computer cannot see, the wave pattern, allows the helmsman to completely fool the machine — just by his normal steering technique.

To make this work, you must alter the helmsman's steering technique, not so much that it makes the whole thing artificial, but enough to solve this problem. The way I have had most success is by asking the helmsman to sail at a specific angle for short periods within the longer test. So if it is an upwind trial then he might start a fifteen minute test by sailing at a target angle of 42 degrees for five minutes. The rule is that he still tries to get the very best out of the boat, but that as close as possible he must stick to that angle. At the end of the five minutes you change the target angle slightly, perhaps to 40 degrees, and then again to 38 degrees for the final five minutes. Doing this seems to give the up-turned U plots that you are looking for, from which you can deduce the target boat speed and angle. Do not forget to record the average wind speed so that you know what wind your target is for!

There is a more efficient way to do all this testing, and it is the method that was so successfully used by the New Zealand *America*'s Cup Challenge in 1987 — two boat tuning. Used by dinghy sailors for years, it exploits the point that we made earlier about a twenty foot gain being an obvious margin when compared to another boat — but the .02 of a knot difference is impossible to measure. You simply sail two boats beside each other that are as identical as they can be in all respects except one — which is the variable being tested. See which boat is faster, swop the variable from one boat to the other and do it again and again. Eventually a pattern will emerge and you can conclude which is the fastest set-up. It is not quite that simple as changes in wind direction will give one or the other boat an apparent advantage, and you must be careful to check that both boats are sailing in the same conditions (Diagram 5.5).

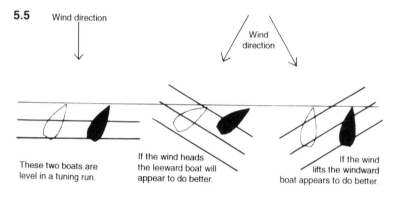

5.5   Wind direction

Wind direction

These two boats are level in a tuning run.

If the wind heads the leeward boat will appear to do better.

If the wind lifts the windward boat appears to do better.

To resolve these problems the full set-up would include a tender following the two boats, with the instrument data from each relayed to it. This can then be analysed to check that the conditions on each yacht are similar. Along with the instrument data comes a precise measure of the boats position. In Fremantle a *Syledis* system was used to measure the position of the boats to within a metre, now Differential GPS makes this sort of accuracy available to anyone who wants to use it. The tender can then calculate who is gaining and losing and with a bit of mathematics will remove the element of advantage given by a wind shift. It is undoubtedly the most effective method of optimising the performance of a sailing boat yet devised.

But of course not all of us have the two boats, tender, telemetry and GPS systems necessary. But that is not to say, particularly if you are sailing one designs, that you could not use this system just by teaming up with someone in your fleet and using them as a regular tuning partner. Dinghies do it all the time, why not yachts?

Instrument Techniques using the Polar Table

Next leg calculations

If you know the position or bearing of the mark it is easy enough to calculate the true wind angle for the next leg, using the sailing wind direction. The polar table allows you to convert this into an apparent wind speed and angle, which is often more useful for sail selection. It is done with the Wind Triangle that the instruments use to calculate the true wind. The polar table gives you the otherwise missing piece of information, the boat speed that you will be doing at that true wind speed and angle.

Referring to Diagram 6.1, you work out the bearing to sail on the next leg, including any correction for tide, and then using the sailing wind direction you can calculate the true wind angle that you will be sailing at. You can assume that the true wind speed will be the same as you are currently reading, or you may even change it to anticipate for some effect that you foresee on the next leg — such as a squall. Then you can look up the boat speed that you will do at this true wind speed and angle in the polar table. Using the boat and true wind velocity vectors you can find the third side of the Wind Triangle, which is the apparent wind speed and angle. If your sailing wind is properly calibrated this apparent wind will also be corrected for upwash, mast twist and so on, and will always be slightly different from the uncorrected values you will read on the boat.

It is a lot easier if you can program a computer or calculator to do all this for you, allowing you just to enter the next leg heading, wind direction and speed. Some instrument systems allow you to enter a course and from this they calculate the next leg data. But obviously the instrument system would have to have an internal polar table that matched your boat, and this is unlikely to be found in anything other than top of the range models. A simpler solution is to make sail selections from true wind angle and speed rather than apparent!

6.1 Next leg calculation

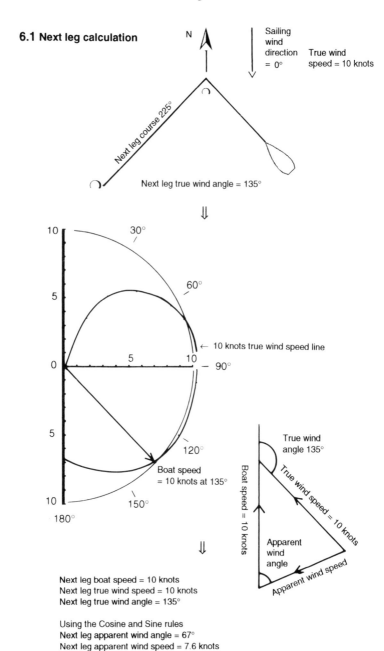

N

Sailing wind direction = 0°

True wind speed = 10 knots

Next leg course 225°

Next leg true wind angle = 135°

⇓

30°

60°

← 10 knots true wind speed line

5

0   5   10   — 90°

5

120°

Boat speed = 10 knots at 135°

10   150°

180°

True wind angle 135°

True wind speed = 10 knots

Boat speed = 10 knots

Apparent wind angle

Apparent wind speed

⇓

Next leg boat speed = 10 knots
Next leg true wind speed = 10 knots
Next leg true wind angle = 135°

Using the Cosine and Sine rules
Next leg apparent wind angle = 67°
Next leg apparent wind speed = 7.6 knots

Velocity made good to the course: VMC

The idea of Vmc, or Velocity made good in the direction of the course, is something you might have come across on your position fixer. It is a simple enough idea, being the net velocity that you are making towards the mark, in the same way that Vmg is the net velocity that you are making towards the wind. It is calculated in a similar fashion, being the velocity that you are making across the ground multiplied by the cosine of the angle between your COG and the course to the mark. As in Diagram 6.2, if X is the angle between your COG and the bearing of the mark then:

$$Vmc = SOG \text{ x cosine } X$$

All these values are available to a position fixer which has a waypoint memory, which is why some of them have started calculating the value for you. Whether or not you should use it is another question altogether.

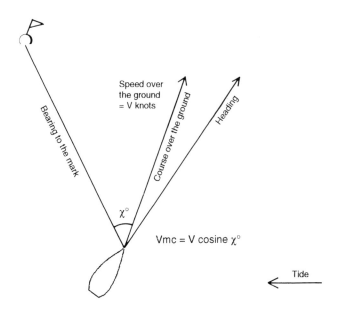

6.2

Vmc is a tactical and strategic tool that helps you follow the general rule, 'Shorten the distance between you and the mark as quickly as possible'. It is most valuable when you have no idea what the weather or the current is likely to do. If the geographical effects on the leg you are about to sail are, to all intents and purposes, random, then your best chance is to keep taking the option that gets you closest to the mark. Whatever the weather throws at you, you have the least distance possible to sail — even if it is directly upwind! The point to bear in mind is that there is almost always a faster way to sail the leg than by just optimising the Vmc. The way to achieve this is to predict correctly the effects up the leg and then position the boat to make the best use of them. We will look at one approach to this in the next section. But first there are a couple of points that we should make; optimising your Vmc on a reaching leg may not mean sailing straight at the mark, and secondly, optimum Vmc upwind is not necessarily the same as your optimum Vmg.

Taking the reaching leg example first, it may sound rather far fetched to say that you can close on the mark faster by not sailing on the direct line towards it, but it all depends on the shape of the polar curve (Diagram 6.3). Some polar tables have a pronounced bump that allows the extra speed gained by going faster and away from the mark to make up the extra distance sailed (Vmg sailing works on exactly the same principle). You would be right in asking the obvious question, if you start by sailing off at an angle to the course how do you eventually get to the mark? The answer is that as you sail down the leg, the Vmc course and the course to the mark converge until they are the same. You end up sailing a loop to the mark. Whether this loop is faster in total than just sailing the rhumb line would depend on the exact detail of the polar table, and you will probably need a computer to work it out.

Sailing to optimise Vmc is really only going to work where the leg is a long one and you expect some kind of change to take place. Imagine a situation where you knew the weather was going to change but had no idea how. You sail the optimum Vmc and everybody else goes down the rhumb line. Half way along the leg you are a couple of miles closer to the mark when the wind drops out. There is a few hours of calm before the race starts again with a new wind direction. That couple of miles is then converted into a lead — so long as you are not disadvantaged by the new wind direction compared to the opposition. But given all that we have said about the approximate nature of polar tables, the wisdom of yachting off at a tangent to the rhumb line on a whim of the polar table, does sound rather suspect and I would have to confess that I have never done it.

Which is a good moment to make a point about the use of polar tables for tactical situations like this. Despite all that we have said about the accuracy of polar tables, they do

6.3

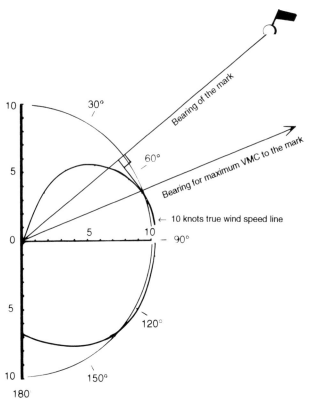

seem to work well in tactical applications. They are not too badly affected by the problems of wind sheer and gradient because they work from the shape of the polar curve more than the exact speed predicted (Diagram 6.4). Wind sheer means that the boat speed achieved at any particular wind angle and speed is inconsistent. But within a wind speed range of 4 or 5 knots the proportion of boat speed to angle, represented by the shape of the curve, is the same. Only extreme conditions of wind sheer will produce a sufficiently big gap between the wind speed at the masthead and the real pressure available to put you into an area of the table where the shape is different. So tactical judgements from polar tables will work reasonably well, despite all the problems.

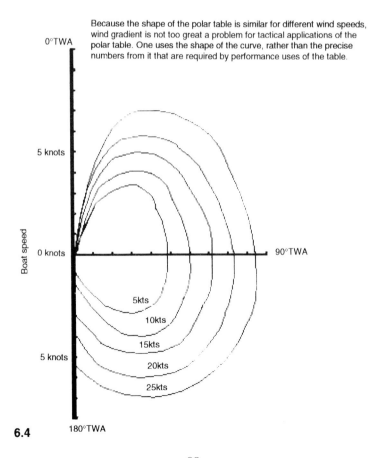

Because the shape of the polar table is similar for different wind speeds, wind gradient is not too great a problem for tactical applications of the polar table. One uses the shape of the curve, rather than the precise numbers from it that are required by performance uses of the table.

6.4

Going back to the reaching leg we had considered earlier, there is an occasion where sailing off-course is highly recommended. This is when the leg is just a little bit too tight to hold a spinnaker all the way down it, so that if you do hoist you will end up low of the mark. The alternative is a two-sail reach all the way down the leg. It is a situation that you come across quite a lot and it is much quicker to put the spinnaker up and hold it as long as you can (Diagram 6.5). You must judge the drop quite carefully so that you come in on a fast two sail reach at the end.

6.5

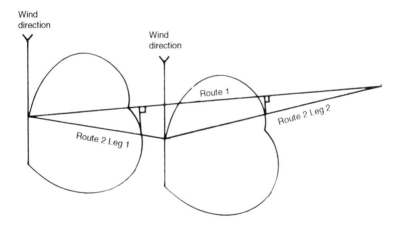

(Drawn to scale)

Route 1 = 14.4nm at 4.1 knots = 3 hours 30 minutes 44 seconds.
Route 2 = 5.6nm at 4.7 knots and 9nm at 4.2 knots = 3 hours 20 minutes 3 seconds.

We can see why the longer course works if we look at the polar table. There is usually a concavity between areas of the curve where the spinnaker is up and areas where you are two sail reaching. This acts in the same way as the concavity in the polar table at upwind and downwind angles. By sailing as high and as fast as you can with the spinnaker and then dropping it and going as fast as you can with two sails up you are effectively 'tacking' down the reach — optimising your Vmg just as you would upwind or downwind. It is a technique well established in the dinghy classes when you cannot lay a gybe mark with the spinnaker up. You then sail high and fast until the angle is such that you can hold the kite and then hoist. Once it is up you can hold it round the mark and onto the next reach, following the same principle when dropping it to make the leeward mark.

Things get even more interesting when we apply the principles of Vmc to the upwind and downwind legs. If we imagine the boat sailing towards the windward mark with the wind blowing directly from the mark and no current then we can see that the optimum Vmg course is the same as the optimum Vmc course (Diagram 6.6a). But if the wind shifts we must rotate the polar table round to line up with the new wind direction. The optimum Vmc and Vmg courses no longer match — we can get to the windward mark faster by sailing at a different angle to the optimum Vmg. If we rotate the wind so that it has lifted us on this tack then we see that we should sail lower and faster to optimise our Vmc to the mark (Diagram 6.6b) and if it heads us then we should sail higher and slower (Diagram 6.6c). If you are going to use this technique you will need a very accurate polar table, right down to the tenths of a knot that each couple of degrees change in wind angle will give you — something that we have already written off as impossible.

Under any circumstances that might be described as normal, I still think that such a precise polar table cannot be developed. But the *America*'s Cup is not a normal situation, and the Fremantle venue of the 1987 event was

6.6

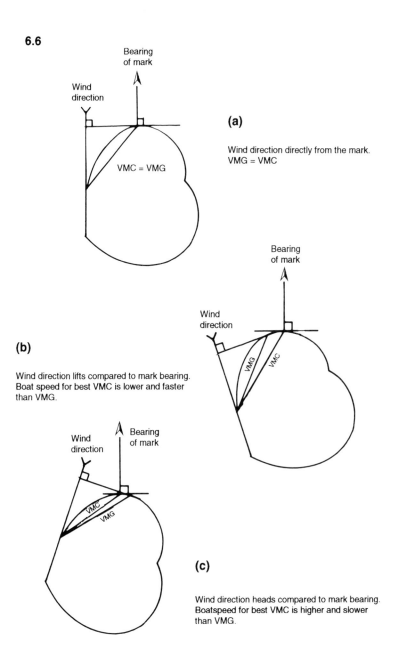

(a)

Wind direction directly from the mark.
VMG = VMC

(b)

Wind direction lifts compared to mark bearing.
Boat speed for best VMC is lower and faster
than VMG.

(c)

Wind direction heads compared to mark bearing.
Boatspeed for best VMC is higher and slower
than VMG.

the key to making it work. The technique was developed by the *Stars and Stripes* team. Not only did they have the time and resources to refine their polar tables to the necessary extent, but they were also blessed with remarkably consistent conditions of wind gradient and sheer. The *Fremantle Doctor* provided the perfect opportunity for this to work, allowing them to sail to a different target speed depending not only on the wind speed but also on the wind direction. So concerned were they that this should not fall into the hands of the other syndicates that there was considerable resistance to the placement of TV cameras on board *Stars and Stripes*. After finally agreeing, they developed a code name for the information to hide its significance. 'Wally' became the boats 'twelfth man', as the 12 Metre computers were so often described by the media.

For the rest of us, without the resources of an *America*'s Cup syndicate or such consistent wind conditions, developing the polar to that extent is just about impossible. Nevertheless the general rules can be applied; sail fast in the lifts and high in the headers. Not by much, perhaps just a couple of tenths on the boat speed dial. You will often find that this agrees with more general tactical rules. If you have sailed out to one side of the course and the fleet, when you get the header to tack back and consolidate, you need to sail and cross as many boats as you can as fast as possible — so you sail fast on the lift that takes you across the fleet. Similarly if you are trapped on a header by a boat to windward that will not tack you can minimise your losses by holding high and slow and letting him sail over you quickly so that you can tack.

Weather and current routing
Weather and current or tidal routing is the ultimate strategic tool, the one way that you can balance the most complex patterns of wind and water flow and come up with a definitive fastest route. There has to be a catch and there is, you need to know what the wind and current will do in advance. In the case of the tide this is not so bad, and tidal

routing has a big future in races where it is well understood — such as the English Channel. The wind is more difficult, whether you are tracking large pressure systems across the Atlantic, or trying to predict a wind bend up the next leg of an Olympic triangle the weather is equally uncooperative. Despite this, weather routing has scored some great successes, particularly on trans-Atlantic races and for the French team in the 1991 *Admiral*'s Cup.

So how does it work? As in Diagram 6.7, we know that the polar table describes the speed at which the yacht will sail at all wind angles, at any particular true wind speed. If we fix the time at one hour it will also show all the places that the yacht can reach in one hour. If, after that hour the wind or the tide changed then a second polar table, rotated to account for the new conditions, could be appended to the first at all points. (Or in practice every ten degrees of true wind angle.) This would then show all the places the boat could reach in two hours. This technique can be repeated as often as you like, though doing it graphically would quickly become unmanageable.

And this is the second catch, you are going to need some serious computer software and hardware to do the job. The commercial systems that are available are expensive and so far their use has been restricted to the grand prix end of the market. But like all computer equipment the price will come down and accessibility will improve — it is in that hope that this section justifies its place in the book. The machines are programmed to repeat the calculation until the expanding wave of 'places the yacht can reach in an equal period of time' overlaps the destination. Then working back through the calculations the optimum route to this point will be given by the angle sailed on each polar table 'leg'. If you follow the computer suggested route you will sail the fastest possible way from A to B — at least that is the theory.

We discussed the implication of polar table errors in the previous section, although in this instance it is a lesser problem than that of the wind and current forecasting.

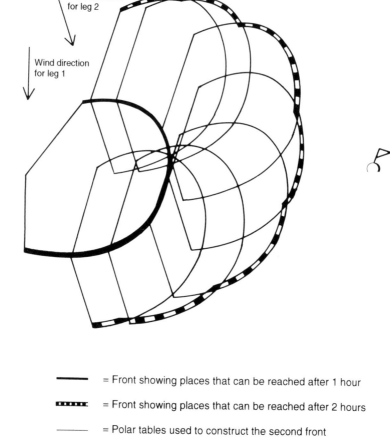

Wind direction
for leg 2

Wind direction
for leg 1

▬▬▬	= Front showing places that can be reached after 1 hour
■■■■■	= Front showing places that can be reached after 2 hours
———	= Polar tables used to construct the second front
	A third front should be constructed to overlap the buoy

6.7

We have already mentioned the problems with the predictions of wind and tide so that the polar table can be set at the right angle for each leg. This is particularly acute for long legs such as those of the Whitbread race. The solution is only of any value if the front of places that you can reach in an equal period of time completely overlaps the destination. For an English Channel passage, or even a seven day sprint across the Atlantic, forecasting to the finish is possible. But a thirty day Whitbread leg sees your weather predictions sliding from the reasonably accurate to the unreasonably hopeful. For the system to work well the operator must have a clear idea of these problems and how they may implicate his decision. The routing becomes a sophisticated 'what if' calculator, allowing you to set up several scenarios and see where they take you. Choosing your course may be a question of balancing the various possibilities and coming up with the lowest risk strategy.

In many ways weather and tidal routing systems epitomise the way the job specification for a navigator has changed in the last few years. It is not necessarily any harder, but it is certainly different. The skills that were formerly involved in keeping the constant plot running on the chart (without an electronic position fixer) are just as difficult to master as the complexities of the modern instrument and computer system. The difference is that the navigator can now contribute a great deal more to the sailing of the yacht — both its performance analysis and the tactics. All the techniques we have looked at can be learned by anyone, with the emergence of commercially available systems with all the functionality of the best Grand Prix equipment. The calibration of the instruments, generation of the polar tables, and then the application of all this to navigational and tactical problems defines one of the most complex roles on a modern race boat. I hope that this book has provided some insight to it.

Index

Other books in the Tips from the Top series

Quarrie on Racing by Stuart Quarrie
Tactics, navigation, sail-trim and crew work explained by one of Britain's top international racing yachtsmen.
ISBN 1 85310 300 4

Cunliffe on Cruising by Tom Cunliffe
Really practical tips to help the cruising yachtsman.
ISBN 1 85310 301 2

Also from *Waterline*

Boatwords by Denny Desoutter
Over 1500 boating terms explained in the author's entertaining style.
ISBN 1 85310 299 7

Hand, Reef and Steer by Tom Cunliffe
Traditional seamanship for classic boats.
Publication March '92
ISBN 1 85310 309 8

Going About Cruising by Andrew Simpson
An introduction to cruising
Publication January '92
ISBN 1 85310 293 8

Write for a complete catalogue of Waterline Books to 101 Longden Road, Shrewsbury, SY3 9EB, England